BRESCIA UNIVERSITY COLLEGE LIBRARY
3 6277 00029481 1
T5-AWK-162

UNIVERSITY COLLEGE
Brescia

Translating Modernism

Translating Modernism

Fitzgerald and Hemingway

Ronald Berman

The University of Alabama Press
Tuscaloosa

The University of Alabama Press
Tuscaloosa, Alabama 35487-0380

Manufactured in the United States of America

Typeface: Minion and Goudy Sans

∞

The paper on which this book is printed meets the minimum requirements of American National Standard for Information Sciences-Permanence of Paper for Printed Library Materials, ANSI Z39.48-1984.

Library of Congress Cataloging-in-Publication Data

Berman, Ronald.
Translating modernism : Fitzgerald and Hemingway / Ronald Berman.
p. cm.
Includes bibliographical references and index.
ISBN 978-0-8173-1647-1 (cloth : alk. paper) — ISBN 978-0-8173-8155-4 (electronic)
1. American fiction—20th century—History and criticism. 2. Modernism (Literature)—United States. 3. Fitzgerald, F. Scott (Francis Scott), 1896–1940—Criticism and interpretation. 4. Hemingway, Ernest, 1899–1961—Criticism and interpretation. 5. Literature, Modern—Psychological aspects. 6. Freud, Sigmund, 1856–1939—Influence. 7. Dewey, John, 1859–1952—Influence. 8. Cézanne, Paul, 1839–1906—Influence. 9. Modernism (Art)—Influence. I. Title.
PS374.M535B4756 2009
813′.509—dc22

2008024439

Chapter 1 first appeared in *The F. Scott Fitzgerald Review* 4 (2005).
Chapter 2 first appeared in *The F. Scott Fitzgerald Review* 6 (2007).
Chapter 5 is reprinted from *The Hemingway Review* volume 27, number 1 (Fall 2007).

This book is dedicated to the memory of friends and mentors: Henry A. Murray and John Crowe Ransom.

Contents

Translating Modernism

Introduction

Landscapes and Ideas

In interviews, letters, book reviews, stories, and novels, F. Scott Fitzgerald referred to other texts. He often evaluated writers and the theories they employed. His own characters live in a world of books and magazines, advertisements and movies. They read and are read to. They hear music from Broadway and sometimes have Hollywood scripts on their minds. If they live in the South, they seem able to raise all of the arguments about civilization in the provinces then appearing in Mencken's *The Smart Set* and *Prejudices.* If they live in the North, they are conscious of Walter Lippmann's voluminous criticism of the Idea of Progress. Ideas are worked out in their lives, and their lives are modeled on them. This was a new possibility, and one of Fitzgerald's great themes is the change in self-conception that occurred in America "sometime between 1910 and 1920."[1] He observed that change and used new explanations of behavior for it.

Research on Fitzgerald's interest in the mind tends naturally to center on the 1930s, when Zelda began a long course of therapy in Europe and then in the United States.[2] Scott became knowledgeable enough to follow her treatment, discuss it with her doctors—and even draw some of his own psychiatric conclusions. Some of what he learned appears in *Tender Is the Night* (1934).[3] But Fitzgerald was from the beginning of his career interested in the workings of the mind. The women of "Bernice Bobs Her Hair" know that men observe them "subconsciously," while a "rebellious" sexual thought refuses to be repressed and surfaces in a dream.[4] Sally Carol Happer experiences "deep terror far greater than any fear of being lost" in "The Ice Palace" (67). "Winter Dreams" are "unconsciously dictated" (220) to Dexter Green—some are deeply transgressive, beginning with the sexuality of a girl eleven years old. It is unsurprising that he should run up "against the mysterious denials and prohibitions in which life indulges" (221). In "The Sensible Thing,"

George O'Kelly defines "what 'nervous' meant." From being "emotionally depressed" in that story (290–91) to becoming emotionally bankrupt in the Josephine Perry story of 1931 (546), Fitzgerald's protagonists are judged by contemporary psychological standards. Anson Hunter is "depressed" (335) also in "The Rich Boy," experiencing anxiety as it is described in "Winter Dreams." In "Jacob's Ladder," after drifting off "into a few hours sleep," Jacob Booth creates an "image" (imago or idealized conception) of the woman he loves. According to psychoanalytic usage, such mental reconstructions repeat the past; and this one is "identical with her old self" recalled (364). "A Short Trip Home" may be a ghost story, but it concerns the limits of the narrator's "sanity" rather than his disbelief (385). In "The Bowl," the idea of character is replaced by the newly current idea of "personality" (401).

There was more than one kind of psychological model. *This Side of Paradise* (1920) followed the great debate on "youth culture." Kirk Curnutt states that readers found it to be authoritative, even diagnostic: "Fitzgerald owed his early success to the fact that adolescent and post-adolescent readers were ripe for fiction that substantiated the newfound confusion and complexity associated with teenage life. . . . Amory's descent into disillusionment and ennui seemed such a confirmation of [current psychology] . . . that the *San Francisco Chronicle* suggested *Paradise* could pass for 'an additional chapter [of] G. Stanley Hall's *Adolescence* or a psychopathological case record.'"[5] There were other possibilities. Here is a persistent motif of Fitzgerald's second novel, *The Beautiful and Damned* (1922):

> somnolence drifting about it like a haze (11). . . . They drifted from letters to the curiosities of each other's day (41). . . . a breeze drifting low along the sidewalk (85). . . . she was resting there as a caught, gossamer feather, drifted in out of the dark (86). . . . night would come drifting down (90). . . . he involuntarily drifted into criticism (92). . . . they drifted into an ancient question-and-answer game (93). . . . days like boats drifting along slow-moving rivers (116). . . . drifting from Pasadena to Coronado (159). . . . Men drifted into them by the devious highways of writing and acting (185). . . . his mind drifted off into one of its characteristic daydreams (187). . . . He had been futile in longing to drift and dream; no one drifted except to maelstroms, no one dreamed, without his dreams becoming fantastic nightmares of indecision and regret (234). . . . He dropped his newspaper, yawned, and let his mind drift off at a tangent (261). . . . They turned the corner and moved lackadaisically up a side street, as if following a drifting cable to which they were attached (267). . . . the drifted fragments of the stars became only

> light (272). . . . You drift apart (337). . . . drifting flotsam (365). . . . He held up a handful of stamps and let them come drifting down about him like leaves (368).[6]

The phrases are contemporary—although they look as if they have been borrowed from lesser Victorian poets. The novel uses the concept of mental inertia provided by public philosophy from William James to Walter Lippmann. In this school of thought, moral character (and even national character) had been construed in psychological terms. James endowed the new century with a seminal distinction between the affirmation of "will" and the mere "spontaneous drift . . . towards repose." The mind, he argued, is naturally evasive and inconsistent. It will never put thought into action without the intervention of a strong and conscious "will."[7] Lippmann's *Drift and Mastery* (1914) developed that thesis.[8] Without the guidance of nineteenth-century institutions—without the authority of family, the dogma of citizenship, or a traditional sense of self—Americans could not direct their own lives, much less national affairs. It was now characteristic, Lippmann wrote, to reject all forms of "responsibility." The mind becomes inert, refuses to make choices.[9] That is why Fitzgerald could apply the term *drift* so pointedly to Tom and Daisy Buchanan as well as to Antony and Gloria Patch. The idea operates in Edmund Wilson as late as 1929: it is, he says, imperative to exert our will against our normal existence of "non-thinking," "non-feeling," and "inertly drifting."[10] Mental life necessarily involved conflict, not repose or—as Fitzgerald memorably put it in *The Great Gatsby*—retreat into our diminished selves.

By the time Fitzgerald got to Daisy Buchanan he was able to argue more convincingly than any of his contemporaries that the operation of mind was systematic in all its ventures into speech and act—and also in its hesitancies, withdrawals, indirection, inflections, and disguises. Even before that, in "Winter Dreams," he brought to bear his own thoughts on Freudian psychology, and I have that story particularly in mind.

Hemingway's characters are troubled by the past, but it does not become part of their dialogue. The opposite is true of Fitzgerald's best stories. "Babylon Revisited" and "Winter Dreams" are layered with memories and weave the past into the present. Necessarily, like "Winter Dreams," they break into episodes based on units of time. There are two large patterns governing the story, one simple and the other impenetrably complex. The first of these shows Dexter Green's life as it proceeds on a straight line. His success encounters no obstacles, which is rare in actuality but not when life is seen through the Idea of Progress. In 1922, the year this story was published, Walter

Lippmann identified some particular American dreams: "the country village will become the great metropolis, the modest building a skyscraper, what is small shall be big, what is slow shall be fast, what is poor shall be rich." All things are connected, and, Lippmann adds, individual destinies are understood to "accord with . . . progress."[11] But his linear model does not explain the Gordian nature of experience—for example, the mysteries and prohibitions of Fitzgerald's story. I don't mean only the hidden personality of Judy Jones or even Dexter's mixed feelings for her, but his consciousness of past and future selves.

Fitzgerald had ready access to contemporary ideas of mentality. Both H. L. Mencken and Edmund Wilson wrote about Freudian psychology before and during the early twenties. Mencken had made his reluctant peace with psychoanalysis before Fitzgerald began serious writing. In 1918, he wrote in *The Smart Set* that Freud's theory was now clearly "the youngest of the arts and sciences." Mencken was convinced that the idea of the "subconscious" was a new explanation for human behavior, and that it should be applied to literature. He mentioned especially the discovery that past feelings refused to be "obliterated"—they were never more than temporarily absent from our present thoughts. That led him to other conclusions: "the fact that a good many such throttled memories must be sexual in character is so obvious that it scarcely needs statement. Under our Christian civilization, the sexual impulse is constantly under suppression. Our whole culture, in fact, is largely a conspiracy against it. Not only is it opposed outwardly by a host of social taboos, most of them in conflict with nature; it is also opposed inwardly by powerful concepts of morals and decorum."[12]

I am as much concerned with Freud's thoughts about writers as with writers who thought about Freud. As a critic, Freud is best known for his work on Shakespeare and on high culture. However, he also studied popular fiction, what he described as "novels, romances, and short stories," that endlessly retold the great motif of success.[13] The fiction of success in business satisfied the aspirations of its readers; and it revealed something about writers. Freud thought that they had a unique means of rectifying experience: they could in fiction impose dreams upon the actual pattern of their lives. That was why fiction had so many elements of autobiography, and why it could be judged by the principles of psychoanalysis.

What were the common features of such fiction? Not only the rise from poverty to wealth but the expression of resentment. Freud took as his subject a typical figure in the imagination of industrial democracy, a young man with more talent than money. His memory would have many slights to overcome. He would in "success" stories be led to resolve them through marriage to a rich and beautiful young woman with all the wealth, power, and stability absent from his own life. He needs to marry her not only because she is desirable but because she is symbolic. The story of success is then not only about social mobility. For Freud, it involves a change of self and the quest for an object that can magically resolve the lifelong problem of not having succeeded at all.

Fitzgerald adopted certain ideas but, equally important, he knew when to modify or even to reject them.[14] The circumstances of writing *The Great Gatsby* are revealing. Fitzgerald knew before it appeared that many reviewers would want his book to represent our national life. His introduction to the 1934 reprint of *The Great Gatsby* stated that a given critic might have "twelve different variant aspects of the social scene" on his mind and expect the novelist to deal with all of them.[15] A notable critic, Van Wyck Brooks, had a program of his own. Brooks instructed writers not to become expatriates so that they could get to know their own country. The nation, in fact, was to be their designated subject. Literature might then renew its contact with the national past; writers might with some moral authority confer blame for the business culture and praise for the youth culture. But Fitzgerald thought that there had been too much recent fiction with a purpose. Just after the first edition of *The Great Gatsby,* he responded to Marya Mannes, who thought that novels should be optimistic about youth and praise "the fresh, strong river of America." The idea was, he said, as silly as the phrase.[16] In the Modern Library reprint of *The Great Gatsby* he stated that the novel hadn't sold because its "pages weren't loaded with big names of big things."[17] His most notable reaction was to the philosophy behind the utilitarianism of critics. In a letter to Max Perkins in 1925, he stated that it was impossible to believe in a stable national culture because history was not static—national experience was so various that it was impossible to summarize. And in a letter to Brooks shortly after, he stated flatly that there had never been a single "American scene."[18] That proved to be one of the most useful heresies of the decade.

Brooks and his disciples wanted a national literature, but they had blundered into a philosophical dilemma. George Santayana had pointed out that realities and ideas about them proceeded at different speeds. One might well have a theory about America, but it could be only momentarily or partially valid because there were too many American subjects for a single thought.[19] Within a few years, the Brooks thesis was overturned, and not necessarily by modernism. Ideas about representation were challenged by Alfred North Whitehead, John Dewey, and Walter Lippmann. *Public Opinion,* Lippmann's most famous work, is uncompromising: "public affairs . . . remain dull and unappetizing, until somebody, with the makings of an artist, has translated them."[20] So, too, is Dewey's *Experience and Nature,* which states that "the conscious life of opinion and judgment" should not displace the natural subjects of fiction. The real work of novels, poetry, and plays is to express perception.[21] Robert Westbrook comments that "the capacity to invest nature with meaning was, by Dewey's lights, the jewel in the crown of man's estate."[22] Dewey repeatedly stated that experience was not intelligible until its artistic statement—and Fitzgerald wrote to Max Perkins that he, Hemingway, and Wolfe found it sufficient in their novels "to recapture the exact feel of a moment in time and space."[23] That is certainly Dewey, although modified by echoes of Einstein.

Literary formulations have a long shelf life. One of the most interesting current books on Fitzgerald is a memoir from the Middle East. Azar Nafisi, an Iranian intellectual, taught *The Great Gatsby* in her university class in Tehran as if it were a defendant on trial. She organized her students into a prosecution and a defense. The prosecution was enthusiastic because the book all too accurately represented Western culture, the real defendant in the trial. It was found to demean marriage and the family; its hero was dishonest; it provided no models of civic virtue. In fact, it ennobled adultery. It was only natural for its opponents to say, "This book is supposed to be about the American dream, but what sort of dream is this?"[24] That seems moralistic but covers much of the same ground as early reviews of *The Great Gatsby* in 1925. I have reviewed these on the way to other alternatives. If we are to go by Dewey and Whitehead, the novel has more on its mind than public issues. It persistently asks how we perceive nature and object.

Fitzgerald's novel was written while he was in the country of modernism, among intellectuals to whom the visual arts were supremely important. Like Hemingway, he was acutely conscious of new kinds of description. *The Great Gatsby* refers often to what the Museum of Modern Art identifies as a main subject of modernism, "Common and Uncommon Things."[25] From Cézanne to Picasso and especially in the early twenties, art opened up onto stage sets, installations, and multiple compositions containing an infinite number of perceived things like guitars, bowls, cigarette boxes, flowers, glasses, pitchers, plates, windows—even words made into more graphic forms of art. "The isolated object" did work outside of "narrative."[26] Many of these objects were man-made. Almost all were concerned with industrial production. They had dual identities, appearing first, as it were, in the flesh, then in photographs, drawings, and advertisements. They were—as Picasso observed—especially to be identified with American industrial design. Those social critics who instructed Fitzgerald to image his social world managed to ignore his authoritative depiction of it in terms of the daily perception of sound, sight, and form. I note that John Dewey is now echoed by the Museum of Modern Art's *ModernStarts,* which states that things exist in the mind only after being "reimagined by the artist."[27]

It may be that there is a specific source for such ideas in both Fitzgerald and Hemingway. Gerald Murphy, who worked with Picasso and with Léger, helped to translate their interest in independent forms. Recent scholarship on Murphy and the propagation of ideas in the twenties (*Making It New: The Art and Style of Sara and Gerald Murphy*) concludes that he was consciously involved in a project linking visual and other arts: "his paintings were embodiments of Americanism, celebrating the functionality and power of the machine and partaking of the clarity of modern advertising." This book cites contemporary criticism (1926) of those new subjects of modernism: the "skyscrapers, billboards, and tabloids of New York," linking them to Murphy and the extraordinary minds in his circle.[28]

There was one subject that Murphy learned from Fitzgerald. "I know now," he wrote in 1935, "that what you said in 'Tender is the Night' is true. Only the invented part of our life—the unreal part—has had any scheme any beauty."[29] That statement is deeply personal, and we don't want to draw from it conclusions that go too far from the circumstances. I think, though, that we can detect a subject already familiar to both men. Identity itself is a form of invention.

Fitzgerald had for a number of years, since his first published stories, been deeply concerned with self-conception. His characters literally invent their identities, using authorial words like "tell," "truth," and "story" when describing their lives. These terms contradict each other: the more that "truth" is mentioned, the more uncertainties appear. In "The Offshore Pirate," Curtis Carlyle (his assumed name) says to Ardita Farnum that he is about to tell her the truth about himself—although the life he describes is based on literary models of rise, success, and disillusion. Is his "invented" life more real to him than that of the real Toby Moreland? Knowleton Whitney in "Myra Meets His Family" tells Myra the "truth," but she realizes that he may not recognize it more than this once. Identities don't have inherent boundaries: Benjamin Button says that he doesn't know "*exactly*" who he is, while Judy Jones takes Dexter Green on probation after trying to find out who he is, anyhow. Ailie Calhoun in "The Last of the Belles" reinvents her past every Saturday night. Jay Gatsby promises to tell Nick Carraway God's truth, but there is not much of his own in the statement. As for others in a novel with innumerable autobiographies and biographies, telling all reveals something—but not the truth.

"Story" and "truth" are the subjects of Wallace Fowlie, who has written that all life stories are forms of fiction. Autobiography uses the same devices as the novel. There are not only structural similarities like admission, confession, narration, and recall but also recurrent images and themes.[30] Paul Fussell adds that writers create fiction even when they write travel books.[31] Going back to 1925, the Modern Library edition of William James included a number of pieces on American self-conceiving. Their burden was that we have as many selves as there are people to whom we reveal them.[32] Going far past that date, Patricia Meyer Spacks cites Goethe's remark that "a fact of our life" matters not because it is true but because it is "significant."[33]

Fitzgerald created alternate selves from the arts: actors, dancers, directors, musicians, painters, impresarios. Their careers are paradigmatic, following a pattern of early success and sudden ending. They have adversarial relationships with their audience. They face the same issues as novelists, one particular novelist, in fact. Gordon Sterrett in "May Day" fails at his work just as Fitzgerald begins his marketplace career; while Curtis Carlyle reflects on the penalties of success on Broadway at the same time that Fitzgerald imagines selling out like Booth Tarkington. Even Jim Powell in "Dice, Brassknuckles & Guitar" must adjust to his marketplace. Fitzgerald's stories about entertainment (we think of the relationship of Miles Calman in "Crazy Sunday" to the insipid standards of his "industry") are self-referential. Hollywood was on his mind for a long time: his 1924 essay "The Most Pampered Men in the World" has a strongly felt connection to the work of Charlie Chaplain, Von Stroheim, and De Mille.[34] I think that Fitzgerald describes his own trajectory when he defends the manuscript of *The Last Tycoon:* "Thalberg has always fascinated me. His peculiar charm, his extraordinary good looks, his bountiful success, the tragic end of his great adventure. The events I have built around him are fiction, but all of them are things which might very well have happened, and I am pretty sure that I saw deep enough into the character of the man so that his reactions are authentically what they would have been in life. So much so that he may be recognized—but it will also be recognized that *no single fact is actually true.*"[35] The facts matter, but no more than the strongly implied connections between writer and subject, selves and creativity. The self requires both authorship and directing. Two decades earlier, Edmund Wilson had written some prescient verses about Fitzgerald's drunkard's holiday when he briefly returned to Princeton for a reunion in 1920. He antagonized his classmates because he was drunk and arrogant—but the ultimate problem was that he needed, here as always, to "interpret himself" against an audience.[36] A main point of "My Lost City"—"we scarcely knew anymore who we were and we hadn't a notion what we were"—was the temporality of self.[37]

~

The best information about Hemingway's ideas comes from his texts. After that, there are his acknowledgments of debts to writers he has read and known and to artists whose paintings are important for his own work. I am thinking especially of his allusions to the work of Paul Cézanne. When Hemingway mentions Cézanne, he invokes technique rather than meaning. The two, we know, are inseparable, but Hemingway's statements emphasize tactics: how something is done and what it looks like. One complication about going back nearly a century is that meanings change every few years. Hemingway's ideas about landscape need to be restored and updated because even this early into the twenty-first century, there has been yet another revaluation of Cézanne and postimpressionism. If anything, he occupies a more central place in modern art than we once thought. Art historians have gone back to the circumstances of his life, his background, and his ideas.[38] Research on "the Cézanne effect" connects it to all the arts of modernism because he "*contains everything*."[39] Cézanne's career provided a model: like Hemingway, he did his work away from centers of power; his reputation grew against the critical grain; he outstripped his competition; and he redefined his art. He was often accused of committing the same offenses as Hemingway and provided a biographical legend ready-made. Cézanne's drawings and paintings were unsentimental. They did not refer themselves to "a combination of beautiful things well grouped in nature."[40] They did not even claim to be accurate representations, as in the case of Monet, who refused to call his landscape of Le Havre a "view" because he knew that it would not be recognizable. (E. H. Gombrich put the matter this way: in van Gogh and Cézanne, "the elements of landscape . . . bear as much relationship to a surveyor's record as a poem bears to a police report.")[41] From the late nineteenth century on, it was understood that landscape showed "the artist's subjective engagement with nature's fleeting effects."[42] Instead of a gallery view of a known subject, landscape became bound up with modernism. It became less objective, less utopian, less of a narrative, less illustrative, less of a moralized view of human figures and values. Modernist landscapes referred not overtly to issues but to themselves.[43] It would be wrong to say that they had no point of view because current art history rests on an interpretation of Cézanne's personal and historical ideas as well as his technique. But we will want to concentrate first on things as Hemingway saw them: light, color, and form.

In one of Hemingway's sustained passages on landscape, the arrival in northern Spain in *The Sun Also Rises,* certain phrases are repeated, among them "brown mountains" and "green plain." He does not differentiate tones: seeing only a "sudden green valley. . . . squares of green and brown mountains. . . . a rolling green plain, with dark mountains beyond it. . . . The green plain stretched off."[44] Color dominates while planes, edges, and "the margins of represented objects are irregular but pictorially effective."[45] Such a refusal to map landscape pleased both Braque and Picasso immensely, the former of whom worked on a subject (landscape and seashore at *L'Estaque*) made famous by a Cézanne painting and the latter who owned it. What mattered was fidelity to perception, not to previous certainties. As to color, art historians emphasize the strict limits of Cézanne' palette and his reiterations. Kenneth Clark describes landscapes dominated by "pale greens, earth colours."[46] Max Raphael calls Cézanne's *Le Mont Sainte-Victoire vu des Lauves* a study in "ocher, and green" that contains "brighter and darker greens" broken by verticals and horizontals.[47] Hemingway describes the interruption of "red roofs" at Burguete in Spain: Raphael cites those "red roofs" that Cézanne painted in Provence; Cézanne writes about "red roofs against the blue sky" that he included in his paintings of the Mediterranean coast.[48]

Hemingway's description of the Irati River has a more than geographical connection to his northern Michigan scenes. There are "thick woods . . . dark with trees" that border the road, run along the mountains, line the swamps, create light-filled clearings for the imitative forms of underbrush.[49] They provide a geometrical structure for each view. Here are two passages, the first from "Big Two-Hearted River: Part I" and the second from *The Sun Also Rises:*

> The trunks of the trees went straight up or slanted toward each other. The trunks were straight and brown without branches. The branches were high above. Some interlocked to make a solid shadow on the brown forest floor. Around the grove of trees was a bare space. . . . The trees had grown tall and the branches moved high, leaving in the sun this bare space they had once covered with shadow.[50]

> We walked on the road between the thick trunks of the old beeches and the sunlight came through the leaves in light patches on the grass. The trees were big, and the foliage was thick.[51]

The only sense involved is vision, which suggests translation from the medium of painting. The Max Raphael study of Cézanne's landscape echoes

Hemingway's terminology. Subjects vary in intensity and magnitude; lines go in "all the main directions—the vertical, the horizontal, and many slanted ones; all tendencies to movement—reclining, standing, and extending; every sort of positioning on the surface and opening up in depth, and every kind of transition from rest to movement." Violent contrasts of form and color suggest meanings for which expository action is not required.[52] In Hemingway there is unstated conflict between light and shadow, foliage and earth, growth and obstacles to it.

Terms like *unity, harmony,* and *order,* when used to describe postimpressionist paintings, refer to the arrangement and coexistence of forms and colors. They also refer to what Bill Gorton says—"this is country"—when he walks the forest of the Irati. Bill admires the disposition of things, but he also knows that design has meaning. Meyer Schapiro described Cézanne's work as "an ordered whole," and many critics, following him, have acknowledged meanings beyond technique.[53] I have been especially interested in the connection between formal and metaphorical meanings. *The Sun Also Rises* and the northern Michigan stories are about as far down on any list of writings referring to "order" or "harmony" as can be imagined. But in their landscapes are ideas translated from painting that address "the wish for integration" that landscape composition implies.[54]

Because Hemingway's northern Michigan stories are known to be biographical, we take them also to be representational. The Web sites of towns in this area assure us that the Nick Adams stories took place there, and they have in a concerted way identified locations, views, and even buildings mentioned by Hemingway in his letters and fiction. They assume that experience has been accurately stated. But that can't be the case—many of these stories were written in Paris under the influence of James Joyce and Gertrude Stein. When Hemingway mentions his attempt to describe landscapes he connects it to the techniques of postimpressionism. His landscape of northern Michigan is just as much of an imaginative construct as his landscapes of northern Spain. Ideas about the interpretation of landscape in Hemingway's lifetime had long abandoned what Kenneth Clark called "imitation." Summarizing the theme in one of his most influential books, Clark said that what we see is not reproduced but "recreated . . . in our imaginations."[55] It is certainly true that the northern Michigan stories are organized around experience. It is also true that they are generic. Hemingway identified the components of landscape in the Lillian Ross interview. They were the "woods" and the "rocks" envisioned by Cézanne in the painting most closely identified with Hemingway, *Rocks—Forest of Fontainebleau.*[56] One of the most interesting ways of getting at Hemingway's own graphic art is to see how he handles those familiar things. Landscape, after all, had its great originals before Cézanne and even those "early painters" admired by Hemingway.[57] It has roots in the biblical description of the Creation; and it has always been the subject of poetry as well as of the visual arts. The landscapes of Hemingway convey an enormous amount of critical information about particular scenes important to him—and also about the genre itself.

1

Fitzgerald

American Dreams

Fitzgerald's protagonists are intensely self-conscious and try unsuccessfully to explain themselves to others. They try to remake themselves on the basis of ideas about selfhood. In order to make their psychology credible, Fitzgerald used mechanisms of dream and daydream, and suggested layers of complexity beneath the human surface. In realistic stories like "The Sensible Thing" or in fantasies like "The Curious Case of Benjamin Button" his characters experience the depression he so often mentions; in virtually all other stories sexuality causes conflict. That is not to say that fiction before the new psychology was without awareness of such things. But they were newly interpreted. Fitzgerald, like any other writer, needed ideas to verify behavior. The problem was stated by Edmund Wilson in a letter to Allen Tate in 1931: "If . . . Descartes, Newton, Einstein, Darwin, and Freud don't 'look deeply into experience,' what do they do? They have imaginations as powerful as any poet's, and some of them were first-rate writers as well. . . . The product of the scientific imagination is *a new vision of relations*—like that of the artistic imagination."[1]

We already know a great deal about Freud and twentieth-century art, so that there is no point in reinventing the wheel. But it is useful to review Freud's ideas about authorship as well as those governing sexuality and dreams. Peter Gay has provided a chronology: "from the 1920s on," he writes, the new thought overcame its initial opposition and began to permeate not only social science but literature. In the visual arts and in poetry especially, the "unconscious" was invoked in order to authenticate feelings and ideas. Even more noticeable, "literary critics, following the lead of Freud's paper on 'Creative Writers and Daydreaming' and of such psychoanalytic publicists as Ernest Jones and Otto Rank, began working with Freudian ideas to explicate the psychology of the writer, of fictional characters, and of audiences."[2] Gay thought that the numbers of writers influenced by Freud were too large to calculate—his ideas simply became atmospheric.[3] They were also, as Gay puts it, appropriated wholesale. As for writers, Fitzgerald was not above the practice of silent adaptation: his story "The Third Casket" (1924) borrows title and also content from Freud's 1913 essay "The Theme of the Three Caskets." Freud's essay is about Shakespeare; Fitzgerald's story is about Shakespeare as understood by Freud.[4] As for critics, Edmund Wilson announced in 1920 that Freud was now as important to the intellectual life as Darwin. Wilson was especially concerned with the impact of analysis on dreams, American or otherwise: "No idea has made more extraordinary advances in the last few years than the Freudian theory of the indestructibility of spiritual energy—the theory that it is as impossible to annihilate an impulse or desire as to annihilate matter or physical energy and that any attempt to do so amounts merely to a suppression of the impulse, which goes on manifesting itself with equal strength in some disguised form. We meet it so often in fiction. . . . The most important instrument discovered by psychoanalysis . . . was the interpretation of dreams."[5]

Wilson's modernism rested, in part, on his view of unconscious experience and can best be viewed after the twenties in his biographical-literary studies of Dickens and Kipling. Before the twenties, however, H. L. Mencken had devoted considerable thought to problems of the mind. He tolerated the early Freud, liked what he saw of behaviorism, was enthusiastic about *Studies in the Psychology of Sex* by Havelock Ellis.[6] Like Wilson, Mencken believed that the implications of the new psychology were far more than clinical. It "meets the known facts exactly, and interprets them logically, and diligently avoids all the transcendental pish-posh of the past. The process of thought, under this new dispensation, becomes thoroughly intelligible for the first time. It responds to causation; it is finally stripped of supernaturalism; it is seen to be determined by the same natural laws that govern all other phenomena in space and time. And so seen, it gives us a new understanding of the forces which move us in the world, and . . . enormously strengthens our grip upon reality."[7] Mencken understood that the idea of the unconscious was bound to be misused, especially outside of clinical treatment, but he thought the benefits to writing would be incalculable. Here is his blueprint for literature: "On the surface all is quiet, but down in the depths a war goes on, with nature on one side and rectitude on the other, and that war casts its uncomprehended flames and uproars through the whole consciousness, and influences the whole process of thought, and leaves its influence upon every idea, and every emotion and every dream."[8] The heart of the matter is the power of sexuality, and Mencken rated Freud above Adler and Jung because he had built upon a more compelling motivation than any they had described. It was not the only motivation. Mencken grasped early the great opposition that Freud was to develop between individuals and "the discipline that is civilization"—possibly because it figured so largely in his personal life and in his cultural politics.[9] He had two main conceptions of mental life, one of them the monstrous powers of egotism in the individual, the other the collective Rotarian urge against any kind of "free functioning."[10]

Fitzgerald began his professional life within the orbit of Jamesian psychology; he later became absorbed by Freud and other moderns. The important texts had been picked out, the vital elements of the new theory identified. One notes, however, that there was far more in Mencken than could be filed under Brill, Freud, or Jung. His essays constitute a massive attempt to decipher the motives of Americans and to name their resentments. For Mencken, the melting pot was always boiling over; and conflict would never end between the classes, the sexes, and the generations. One of his great images was the democratic mob. When we see Fitzgerald's mob in "May Day"—dominated by primal fears and manipulated by politics—we may be seeing Mencken's ideas applied. Another of his grand conceptions was the dismal failure of the Idea of Progress. There are arguments in Mencken that explain why "Dalyrimple Goes Wrong." But eventually, Fitzgerald's fiction, even his potboilers, will only begin at Mencken's level. He has much to add about internal conflict.

~

"Winter Dreams," usually viewed as a precursor to *The Great Gatsby,* is part of a sequence of stories about poor boys who want to marry rich girls. Many of these stories have been identified in *The Perfect Hour,* James L. West's biography of Fitzgerald and Ginevra King. This book argues convincingly that the Ur-figure for all of Fitzgerald's distant, unapproachable, and sometimes deadly women was in fact Ginevra, whom he knew, loved, and lost before meeting Zelda Sayre. The relationship, from 1915 to 1917, was briefly reciprocal. Ginevra ended it for a number of reasons, which may have included money and social class, although her letters indicate other causes. She saw that Scott would have been a slippery catch: egotistical, vain, and, in the way of writers, apt to turn those he knew into those he wrote about. She worried a good deal about his reliability and she made the same kind of decision about marriage that Zelda was to make in the spring of 1919. Inevitably, Scott's version has taken pride of place: for the rest of his life she was his great disappointment. Ginevra became the cold-hearted Kismine of "The Diamond as Big as the Ritz" and the man-eater Judy Jones of "Winter Dreams."[11]

Ginevra's letters published by West lead us to Fitzgerald's novels and stories. But they do so in unexpected ways. For one thing, they have more to say about mind than money. Their vocabulary is relentlessly psychological. She is certainly interested in thought—the letters are intelligent and perceptive—but she characteristically describes her *feelings* about those thoughts. The letters analyze her self as seen by others; and they correct the impression that she has no emotional depth. The first of these letters makes a good argument for Ginevra's identification with the narcissistic Judy Jones: with about seventy repetitions of "I" or "me" in some five hundred words. The letter is not about what she is doing but how she feels about it. Perhaps that is where social class comes in because she assumes that she matters without being measured against what she does. Now and then she deals with experienced events, but they have no bulk when compared to "the inner workings of my mind." In one line—"I *know* I am a flirt and I can't stop it"—the first phrase needs to share its emphasis because the second is where the meaning resides.[12] It has little to do with being rich or young or unattainable. These words correspond to the psychological moment. Is she as solipsistic as Judy Jones? The letter exists in response to Fitzgerald's particular urgings and accusations. He was manipulative and provoked her into self-examination. Nevertheless, she explains herself through reference to feelings, guilt, states of mind, norms and aberrations. These things are stated in the lingua franca of the world after Freud.[13]

Here are some of the attitudes she has picked up in Chicago or at Westover School—or from Fitzgerald:

> I didn't care *how* I acted, I liked it, and so I didn't care for what people said—Naturally this was crazy. . . . a girl has to control her feelings, which *is* hard for me. . . . The inner workings of my mind would or would not be of interest to you. . . . nothing under the sun could control our feelings—They're bound to show themselves. . . . You show your ignorance of my nature well. . . . You're crazy! . . . I *say* foolish things sometimes, I am just as liable to write them in my letters—I know, if I ever saw one of my letters again, I would think myself crazy. . . . you said that fine days always depressed you. . . . You seem to feel the same way that I do about being crazy about people, and I suppose it's just human nature to want to own things, only a girl, I think, would rather belong to somebody she loved.[14]

Ginevra is familiar enough with the new language of self-analysis to detect her own self-consciousness and also the practiced melancholia of Fitzgerald. She seems equal to the task of deciphering *him,* especially when she mentions that he would not have kissed her in public because of sexual passion, only because he wanted to be seen doing it. And, that he really has no interest in knowing her but wants her "on a pedestal."[15] That may allude to a familiar Victorian ideal, and also to the frozen pose of a model who responds to instruction. For a woman to be "re-created" by a man's desire is, according to Fitzgerald, to have "lost all vestige" of her own identity.[16]

At some point, Ginevra King is *not* represented by the figures of Kismine Washington, Judy Jones, or Daisy Fay. Writing reconstructs memory. Making a narrative out of biography redistributes facts. That is especially true in a story like "Winter Dreams," which belongs to its own literary subgenre. It is the daydream of a writer who makes his life come out right this time: the obstacles to wealth are removed, and a woman is punished for her disdain by losing her good looks. She passes up the Prince, and marries the Frog.

A more elemental story than that of Scott and Ginevra has been superimposed on this one. It may be approached through Freud's "Creative Writers and Day-dreaming," the essay of 1907 identified by Peter Gay. Unlike Freud's studies of classical literary figures, this is about "the less pretentious authors of novels, romances and short stories" who are "not the writers most highly esteemed by the critics."[17] That is to say, they serve the new mass market of literacy. Freud mentions Zola; our own thoughts will turn to Alger and other American preachers of success. Freud detects a universal sequence in such fiction: starting out poor, changing life by industriousness, marrying a rich girl. No direct influence should be claimed for this essay; I use it because it is the best critique of dreams and daydreams about success at the turn of the century. And of course it identifies an audience, large numbers of men and women in the workforce who were ripe for such literature.

Freud begins by asserting that writers alone can do what the rest of us desire, which is to remake the past. Stories disguising their past are taken very seriously by authors—and such narratives are neither happy nor innocent. That is because a happy person never has fantasies, only "an unsatisfied one." That is confirmed by Fitzgerald in *The Beautiful and Damned:* "no one dreamed, without his dreams becoming fantastic nightmares of indecision and regret."[18] West states that Ginevra King's letters "called into memory the resentments he had felt over slights and snubs, real or imagined. He knew instinctively that much of his best writing came from early feelings of inferiority and failure."[19] In Freud, the protagonists are generic: a "well-brought-up young woman" and a young man with "an excess of self-regard which he brings with him from the spoilt days of his childhood."[20] Childhood has not fulfilled the man's ambitions; it has only left them with him. There are two possibilities: actually getting what he wants (often impossible in the real world) or changing reality. To get what you want you have to change what you are: "Freud defined dream interpretation as a therapeutic rewriting of the dream itself. . . . When Freud warned his readers not to read . . . [a] case history as a novel, he must have recognized how much his presentation of it resembled an act of literary creation. Freud would draw the analogy himself between the recuperation of the subject in his theory of dream interpretation and the construction of a character in any novel when he claimed that 'His Majesty the Ego [is] the hero of all daydreams and every story.'"[21] How far can we go with resemblances to actual lives or, more important, to living art? There is a chilling reductiveness to Freud, especially when we think of the complexity of *The Great Gatsby.* As for "Winter Dreams," we are reminded that "this story is not his biography, remember, although things creep into it which have nothing to do with those dreams he had when he was young."[22] And yet, we need to know about generic narratives. In Freud's account, the present is an opportunity to revive memory of an earlier time when, we think, we once were happy. The *future* matters because it will bring back the past. Those points can't be disregarded. Nor can other similarities. "Let us take the case of a poor orphan boy," Freud says, who succeeds in business and then "marries the charming young daughter of the house."[23] The "house" seems to be as important as the woman. By taking that over, the hero takes control over both his life and that of the woman whose destiny he re-creates. He replaces all other men in her life. In fact, he rewrites her life. Daisy Buchanan, who understands a great deal, knows exactly what wanting "too much" means.

The importance of Freud's essay does not lie entirely in its review of Victorian and Edwardian fiction about love and money. Life is understood to be a matter of drives, enormously potent and sexual. Behavior disguises them. The greater source of conflict is not social but internal: people may have trouble with the social world, but the great issue is that they cannot understand themselves. In an important work of 1925, "An Autobiographical Study," Freud wrote that there really *is* a psychopathology of daily life and its "phenomena are not accidental."[24] Necessarily, the essay renews the effect of *The Interpretation of Dreams.* We prepare ourselves for this kind of narrative by relying less on realism and more on our sense of a pattern governing events. Freud adds: "I was able to show from a short story . . . that invented dreams can be interpreted in the same way as real ones."[25] Fitzgerald was able to show that the "mind" had "its characteristic daydreams."[26] The story that we address is about American dreams—but in their new context.

~

"Winter Dreams" begins on the first tee of a country club where fourteen-year-old Dexter Green refuses to caddy for the impossible eleven-year-old

Judy Jones. They are brought together on the same golf course some nine years later. Dexter now has money; Judy is now impossibly beautiful. She invites Dexter to her home—the largest and most imposing in the area—and he falls hopelessly in love with her. She tolerates him, and he gives up two years of his life pursuing her. But no one can possess Aphrodite. She loves many men; and he understands her nature. Dexter cuts his losses and engages to marry someone else. That decision turns out to make him momentarily irresistible. He and Judy have an affair that lasts a month, ending in final separation. Another seven years pass, and Dexter learns that Judy has married, had children, definitively lost her looks, and is probably beaten by her drunken lout of a husband.

The story is famously about money. There are no mysteries about money—it is the American element—so that this part of the narrative has great clarity. To be poor is to live in a one-room house; to be in the middle of the middle class is to have the second-best grocery in town. Dexter gets rich by starting a "small" laundry that becomes part of "the largest string of laundries in his section of the country" (162). Judy Jones lives in the biggest, most impressive, most elaborate house on Lake Erminie; it won't do for Dexter to wear clothes that aren't made by "the best tailors in America" (168) or even to say more than can be safely identified with Ivy League reticence; Judy Jones says that her father is the best-looking man of his age she's ever seen; Dexter makes the very American statement that "I'm probably making more money than any man my age in the northwest." In Horatio Alger, that would call for accolades. But nothing is simple any longer. When Dexter adds, "I know that's an obnoxious remark" (170–71), we are reminded strikingly of John T. Unger in "The Diamond as Big as the Ritz," a toad who also keeps track of comparatives.

Dexter's career represents the Idea of Progress according to scale. Until the end of the narrative, change is beneficial, one-directional, predictable. He is educated, begins work, makes money, and *encounters no obstacles* to the imposition of a dream pattern on actuality. It was a narrative often retold. For example, in 1920, George Santayana wrote a generic biography of a young American businessman in *Character and Opinion in the United States:* "his ideals fall into the form of premonitions and prophecies; and his studious prophecies often come true. . . . When a poor boy, perhaps, he dreams of an education, and presently he gets an education, or at least a degree; he dreams of growing rich, and he grows rich. . . . He dreams of helping to carry on and to accelerate the movement of a vast, seething, progressive society, and he actually does so." Consequently, "he feels that God and nature are working with him."[27] Fitzgerald used this paradigm often in his stories, and developed it in a newspaper interview of 1926: "Life for Americans from the beginning has been a pursuit, a looking forward; and it may be, because the urge is inherent and ineradicable, that in some field of activity lies their only hope of happiness. The American's happiness is linked with progress."[28] In "Winter Dreams," Fitzgerald's language, slightly orotund, aware of its echoes, matches the solemnity of this national theme: "one day it came to pass" that Dexter's dream took on material form and "he made money. It was rather amazing" (157). It is the language of our civic religion, grateful but expectant.

But there is another kind of language in the story. It refers to things visible but not so easily understood. Dexter has feelings "of profound melancholy" (156), and Judy Jones cannot escape her "moody depression" (170). There are certain mysteries: at a crucial moment, he decides that "there were two versions of his life that he could tell" to Judy (172). He chooses the one that suppresses his identity. That is given up easily in our society—only in philosophy is self-preservation the first law of nature. More important: Dexter has "the sense of being a trespasser" (162) on the far side of the social divide. In fact, the text states that "this story deals" with "mysterious denials and prohibitions" and not with Dexter's career (161). Freud himself in 1915 used the phrase "taboos and prohibitions" to signify things not understood that nevertheless force our repression of feelings.[29] A straightforward story told in terms of time, number, and probability can't explain itself in terms of these quantities.

We know that things are forbidden in different ways and on different scales; we know also that repression is as active as expression. It is a universal taboo to love a girl who has not reached puberty. It is a social taboo to make love to a woman of a different caste—if you happen to be an unemployed writer or, let us say, a gamekeeper. Or if, in Fitzgerald's chronicles of social life, you offend against "family solidarity."[30] It is taboo—and on the biblical scale—to forget your parents, no matter how conveniently. Certain things are presented as social tactics in the story, but they have immense psychic reverberations. Does this story make its effect through romantic disappointment alone? It ends with an extraordinary, drawn-out description of lost illusions. But there may be something even more intellectually compelling. Fitzgerald knew that Mencken had praised Freud in 1918 precisely because the past could not be "obliterated."[31] In 1920, another mentor, Edmund Wilson, had written that "it is as impossible to annihilate an impulse or desire as to annihilate matter or physical energy."[32] The loss of the past affects Dexter as much as the loss of Judy Jones. I think that there are more sorrows in this story than romantic evanescence, and it is as much about America as about dreams.

Dexter Green gives up the conscious past: his parents, background, community. But in order to do that he has to give up something else, the sense of self, which is based precisely on those things. When he meets Judy Jones as an adult he is nervous because of her effect on him—and also because he is considerably less than certain about himself or his self. He says that there are two stories he might tell her—which means that there are two selves for those stories. We may need to reinterpret some of the lines in the story's ending: "For the first time in years the tears were streaming down his face. But they were for himself now. He did not care about mouth and eyes and moving hands. He wanted to care and he could not care. For he had gone away and he could never go back any more" (185). These lines are about Dexter, not Judy Jones: "long ago, there was something in me, but now that thing is gone." The story is much less romantic than it seems. It is not about the prize but what it cost. And this is where the story becomes most American. I think that even if Judy had married him—among the many impossibilities to which the reading mind is subject—that paragraph would still have been written. The Santayana essay that I have cited ends its biography of the successful young businessman with the observation that "the present moment" always seems invulnerable. Yet *something* has necessarily been lost by its arrival. The tension of his essay comes from its gathering doubt—it is highly dramatic—as to whether Americans can be immune to that tragic recognition. So far, he says, we have managed to translate the idea of success from material to human things, to think about the mind the same way we think about success. But there are larger conceptions than progress, one of them being the shock of insolubility.[33]

~

Like Fitzgerald himself, and like many of his characters, Judy tries to keep order by number, allowing a specific number of men in her life, imposing her own schedule on events. She assigns a certain number of days (sometimes hours) to whatever man is momentarily predominant. She certainly imposes categorical ideas:

> "I've just had rather an unpleasant afternoon. There was a—man I cared about. He told me out of a clear sky that he was poor as a churchmouse. He'd never even hinted it before. Does this sound horribly mundane?"
>
> "Perhaps he was afraid to tell you."
>
> "I suppose he was," she answered thoughtfully. (170)

Freud notes that success stories contain much that is shameful. Because they are about dreams, we tend to say things so unguarded that they might never be admitted in waking life. We can see that this dialogue is as "unpleasant" as the experience it describes. Of course the story sounds "mundane"—that is how social judgments are made within our minds. The encounter must have been emotionally difficult for the man, but we hear only one point of view, that of the woman. She could not, she adds, "survive the shock" of his admission, and (this may be why the very rich are not like us) is herself its victim. Dexter knows the rules: when Judy reveals the depth of her solipsism he puts the burden on the man who unwisely told the truth; when she explains how badly she has been wounded he assures her that nothing uncommon has happened. Nothing remains to be said because he already knows that poor men have no right to reasonable explanation.

How real is Judy Jones? Freud advises us not to look for realism in day-dream narratives because there is only one subject: "we can immediately recognize His Majesty the Ego, the hero alike of every day-dream and of every story." There is only one consciousness in the story: "the author sits inside his mind, as it were, and looks at the other characters from outside. . . . the person who is introduced as the hero plays only a very small active part; he sees the actions and sufferings of other people pass before him like a spectator."[34] That raises a difficult issue for the interpretation of narrative as biography. The purpose is not to describe a true experience but to fulfill "a wish . . . in the creative work."[35] And yet, a good critical essay on "Winter Dreams" suggests that there are "real" reasons for Judy Jones being what she is.[36] She is instinctively against male domination. She reacts against social constraint and wants an equal sexual (and even marital) relationship. She may be presumed to have engaged in her own search for rational happiness by giving up "idiotic" social pleasures and by actively seeking out a normative form of love. Her life might have had a happy ending if society were less restrictive, or she had married the right man. My own view necessarily differs. The story is not about her condition but about her nature. When she asks, "Why can't I be happy?" (180), she does not mean "What do I have to do to be happy?"

Her question resonates through the early twentieth century. It was framed as she construes it long before 1922. And it was restated at the end of the twenties, when Freud summed up his research on "the problem of why it is so hard for men to be happy."[37] He had developed his theory of destructive instincts since the turn of the century, notably in *Three Essays on Sexuality* (1905); "Instincts and Their Vicissitudes" (1915); and *Beyond the Pleasure Principle* (1920).[38] In 1923 he did his classic study of love and death, *The Ego and the Id*.[39] All of these works asked why human happiness was not possible; all answered that hatred had a bipolar connection to love. Philip Rieff summarizes one strand of Freud's thought: "within human life aggression may become conscience or cruelty or, mixed in the most delicate combinations and put out to work in familiar ways." This makes "all relations a little more dangerous" than they first appear.[40] Especially when it is understood that destructiveness is directed at *both* object and self.

I think, however, that the most revealing analysis of the problem of sexual happiness appears in Freud's review of his own case histories toward the end of *Beyond the Pleasure Principle.* Here he recalls those love affairs that pass "through the same phases" and reach "the same conclusion" no matter what the actual experience has been like. (He adds, usefully, that his sense of this issue derives also from the literature of love.) Treatment may not be possible for all those, however normal they may seem, who declaim about their unhappiness. Invariably they prefer unhappiness to the loss of power.[41]

Freud returned to the issue in *Civilization and Its Discontents,* which states that we are unhappy because nature acts upon us and thwarts our will, because our bodies are feeble—and principally because "the mutual relationships of human beings" are "the social source of our suffering." Our greatest source of unhappiness is the relationship of the self to its objects. The problems of nature and age may be solved—but unhappiness, self-hatred, destructiveness are all pieces "of our own psychical constitution."[42] Judy Jones is not, I think, true to the biography of Ginevra King, but she is true to the regnant theory of mentality. Freud's conclusion to *The Ego and the Id* appeared the year after Fitzgerald's story and is a wonderful parallel to it: "It would be possible to picture the id as under the domination of the mute but powerful death instincts, which desire to be at peace and . . . to put Eros, the mischief-maker, to rest; but perhaps that might be to undervalue the part played by Eros."[43]

~

A year after writing "Winter Dreams," Fitzgerald said this about a book he despised: "There is a recent piece of trash entitled *Simon Called Peter,* which seems to me utterly immoral, because the characters move in a continual labyrinth of mild sexual stimulation."[44] The book stayed on his mind—two years after that, Nick Carraway reads it in Myrtle Wilson's living room while she and Tom make love in the bedroom. We will see connections, however, rather than distancing: "Winter Dreams" has an atmospheric sexuality that is by no means mild. The story even suggests a labyrinth explored by two lovers. Judy is described in the most skilled and haunting erotic prose that Fitzgerald ever wrote. She is not a symbolic woman like Daisy Buchanan or Nicole Warren:

> The color in her cheeks was centered like the color in a picture—it was not a "high" color, but a sort of fluctuating and feverish warmth, so shaded that it seemed at any moment it would recede and disappear. This color and the mobility of her mouth gave a continual impression of flux, of intense life, of passionate vitality—balanced only partially by the sad luxury of her eyes. . . . Watching her was as without effort to the eye as watching a branch waving or a sea-gull flying. Her arms, burned to butternut, moved sinuously among the dull platinum ripples, elbows appearing first, casting the forearm back with a cadence of falling water. . . . three days of long evenings on her dusky verandah, of strange wan kisses through the late afternoon, in shadowy alcoves or behind the protecting trellises of the garden arbors, of mornings when she was fresh as a dream and almost shy at meeting him in the clarity of the rising day. (163–73)

It is like reading *The Leopard* of Lampedusa, which tells of making love in silent rooms within a building that itself suggests prohibited entry. Fitzgerald will signify sexual experience by the opening and closing of a bedroom or entry door. His tactics are Freudian: the story is full of images of water, darkness, enclosed gardens, and inaccessible buildings. The maiden's castle is on the edge of the lake. "To the innocent eye," Freud writes in *The Interpretation of Dreams,* a landscape will look like a map. But it is only when we think of the body that it becomes "intelligible." (One of his chapter headings is "The Male Organ Represented by Persons and the Female Organ by a Landscape.")[45] There are different kinds of indirectness: we know from *The Great Gatsby* the probable meaning of "the corners of her mouth drooped until her face seemed to open like a flower" (171).

Ginevra King may have given Fitzgerald's story more than its social themes. Here is a passage from a letter she wrote in 1915: "Your view is ridiculous—Just because you and I—for we are remarkably alike—just because you and I happen to be 'fresh' (excuse me) and have more emotional feeling than most other people have, we're bound, simply *bound* to let it out some way, sometime: and nothing under the sun could control our feelings—They're bound to show themselves—You know you cant [*sic*] *help* falling madly for a girl. It isn't really *you* yourself that does it, it's an indescribable thing inside of you."[46] This was written before H. L. Mencken described the operation of the unconscious as "a war in the depths . . . with nature on one side and rectitude on the other." It would be hard to find a clearer statement of the imbalance between ego, superego, and id. "Winter Dreams" is a more complex story than it appears: a recollection, a biography in spite of itself, a revengeful daydream, a story about poor boys and rich girls—and also a story whose object has provided a theory of human nature. That theory is of course derivative, but long familiar even by the early twenties. The qualities of "wisdom" and "convention," always on Dexter's mind, seem dominant, but finally disappear (181). They are, as the story puts it with great psychic accuracy, sediment buried by water.

2
Fitzgerald
American Realities

In the 1970s, Azar Nafisi, an Iranian graduate student at the University of Oklahoma, began to live a schizophrenic intellectual life. On the political left, she was yet unable to stop loving those counterrevolutionary writers Jane Austen, Nabokov, Fitzgerald, and Hemingway. For a while, the conflict was internal. She then returned to Tehran, now the reformed capital of an Islamic republic, in order to begin her teaching career. After the shah had been deposed, however, reform took an unexpected turn. Women were forced to wear the veil; publications were closed down; intellectuals who went to meetings were sent to jail. There were show trials, and dissenters from the regime began to disappear. Copies of *The Great Gatsby* and *A Farewell to Arms* disappeared as the new government blocked distribution of foreign books in Iran. Nafisi assigned *The Great Gatsby* to her first university class although the choice seemed dangerously political. Most things were: here is a warrant for execution citing the crime of "being Westernized, brought up in a Westernized family; staying too long in Europe for his studies; smoking Winston cigarettes."[1]

The class was instructed to treat *The Great Gatsby* as if it were a defendant on trial. A willing prosecutor, Mr. Nyazi, argued that Fitzgerald should never be read because his work—his very subject—was indecent:

> "The only sympathetic person here is the cuckolded husband, Mr. Wilson," Mr. Nyazi boomed. "When he kills Gatsby, it is the hand of God."
>
> "The one good thing about this book," he said, waving the culprit in one hand, "is that it exposes the immorality and decadence of American society, but we have fought to rid ourselves of this trash and it is high time that such books be banned." He kept calling Gatsby "this

> Mr. Gatsby" and could not bring himself to name Daisy, whom he referred to as "that woman." According to Nyazi, there was not a single virtuous woman in the whole novel. "What kind of model are we setting for our innocent and modest sisters," he asked his captive audience, "by giving them such a book to read?"
>
> As he continued, he became increasingly animated, yet he refused throughout to budge from his chair. "Gatsby is dishonest," he cried out, his voice now shrill. "He earns his money by illegal means and tries to buy the love of a married woman. This book is supposed to be about the American dream, but what sort of a dream is this? Does the author mean to suggest that we should all be adulterers and bandits? . . . This is the last hiccup of a dead culture! . . . What kind of a dream is it to steal a man's wife, to preach sex, to cheat and swindle and to . . . and then that guy, the narrator, Nick, he claims to be moral!"[2]

Nyazi has an interesting take on Wilson because both are wrong in the same way. Yet not all the ironies of this passage are safely indulged. Meyer Wolfshiem also admires "the kind of man you'd like to take home and introduce to your mother and sister."[3] Nyazi is wrong about Gatsby, whom he has confused with Elmer Gantry, although he may be right about Nick.[4] He ends his prosecution of the novel with this question: "Why doesn't Mr. Gatsby get his own wife?" Nicely trumped by a witness for the defense: "Why don't you write your own novel?"[5] A number of questions raised in this passage belong to the history of criticism of the twenties.[6]

Some of the questions at this trial were reincarnations.[7] Grant Overton's review of *The Great Gatsby* in *Collier's* stated that the novel was a perfect picture of national life understood through tabloid headlines. He seems to have copied his metaphors from an earlier reviewer, Isabel Paterson, who had in the *New York Herald Tribune Books* described the major characters as a kind of "froth of society." By the time it reached him, Overton drew out every figurative implication from the bubbles and scum left by incoming waves to that "froth" leftover that was a correlative for American social life. Both reviewers thought that the distressing subject of the novel—easy money in New York—had been made bearable by its style. Both stuck to the issues of social class and public morality as if these things defined the meaning of novels.[8] The *New York Sun* reviewer Herbert S. Gorman wrote that the novel was about "an unstabilized and decadent society." Its view of "this contemporaneous life" could not be morally justified. Walter Yust in the *New York Evening Post Literary Review* summarized the story as one of "polite corruption." It covered "a portion of society that embodies disillusion." Attacking from the other side of the public morality argument, Harvey Eagleton, the reviewer for the *Dallas Morning News,* worried about "the omission of the constructive in Fitzgerald's work." In brief, *Gatsby* should have been socially prescriptive. There were some sharp and even brilliant journalistic remarks by Thomas Caldecot Chubb, William Rose Benét, and Gilbert Seldes, the last of whom noted that *Gatsby* offered more to think about than "the outside of American life."[9]

~

Many novels of the twenties raise such issues. Edmund Wilson was not immune—here is a doctrinal moment from *I Thought of Daisy.* Hugo Bamman, who combines aspects of both Wilson and John Dos Passos, is thinking about life and letters in America:

> And so he walked among us like a human penance for the shortcomings of a whole class and culture—of the society which, in America, had paralysed in his friends and himself half the normal responses to life; which had sterilized its women with refinements; which had lived on industrial investments and washed its hands of the corruption of politics; which had outlawed its men of genius. . . . In the America where Hugo came to manhood, there was, in a sense, only a single class and a single culture; one found it behind every façade, one felt it through every uniform—and not merely among those members of society whom it had already become fashionable to ridicule: the small business man, the hired reformer, the windbag politician—but in the cramped mind of the clever lawyer, for whom intellectual dignity and freedom had been forbidden by the interests which he served . . . even in the universities, with their presidents held in subjection by millionaire trustees, with their middle-class timidity about raising, in class or conversation, the real political, moral, or aesthetic problems of the time.[10]

I have elided liberally: Wilson also mentions labor leaders, physicians, evangelicals, self-made men and, especially, literary critics: all guilty of having come to terms with national life. While Fitzgerald was trying to write the Great American Novel, Wilson, Van Wyck Brooks—even Mencken—were looking for a great novel about America.[11]

Fitzgerald had foreseen the attitudes and theories of reviewers. He understood their *affaire* with social class, writing to Max Perkins on the day *Gatsby* came out that critics would dislike it "because it dealt with the rich." A long, satirical letter to Perkins in June 1925 noted that novelists suffered from a bad case of agrarian virtue, idolizing the "typical American material" of farmers working piously on the land. In October, he told Marya Mannes that she had a false idea of the "fresh, strong river of America" informing his fiction.[12] Such critical sentimentality ensued because both Mencken and Brooks, the two most influential men of letters before *Gatsby,* had provided reviewers with a vocation of addressing society through literature. For this mindset, modernism was ideologically useless. But the letter to Perkins in June showed Fitzgerald's new relationship to criticism: the literary vocation of Americanism was "*stubborn seeking for the static in a world that for almost a hundred years has simply not been static.*"[13] Whatever novels were, they were not about social orders like the one defended by Brooks.

Fitzgerald's obit in the *New York Times,* often mentioned, is more than dismissive, it is inaccurate. The *Times* recognized that he had assumed authority as the voice of the Jazz Age by recording it.[14] But the issues of 1922 were not those of 1929—let alone those of 1940. The decade moved quickly, and Fitzgerald understood that it was not an integrated whole. There is a discorrelation between his work and the world as understood by critics from 1920 to 1940. In fact, when *The Great Gatsby* appeared, Fitzgerald was thought to be insufficiently informed about his times. He wrote about too small a statistical sample of people; he stuck to a single social class; he tackled no important national categories such as "Youth" or "Business." Van Wyck Brooks thought that Fitzgerald could not be an important novelist because he failed even to describe the twenties in America. The following is fairly definitive: "There was no touch of the American language in the tales of Scott Fitzgerald, *the typical writer of the twenties, as he seemed later,* whom I saw now and then with the friend of my childhood, Maxwell Perkins, the publisher who regarded him almost as a son."[15] Brooks refused to believe that any expatriate knew enough to write about his own country, which is wrongheaded enough. But he did have a point: in the early twenties, Fitzgerald was not seen as a reliable witness. It was only "later" that the confusion came about.

In "The Delegate from Great Neck" (1924) Edmund Wilson had Fitzgerald speak to Brooks about a different kind of epistemology. Each modern American writer, Fitzgerald argues, has had "his peculiar sense of life, his particular aspect of America, that he succeeded in getting on paper in some more or less vivid form." Each has been deeply and successfully involved "in the life of their own country."[16] I don't think that this was ventriloquism: Fitzgerald wrote to Brooks in June 1925 that he admired *The Ordeal of Mark Twain* and *The Pilgrimage of Henry James.* However, "the American scene has become so complicated & ramified" that no single viewpoint can any longer account for it.[17] There was a not especially hidden meaning to the interchange. According to Brooks, James should have used his novels to uncover "the inadequacy of our social life." He should have centered on "the plight of the highly personalized human being in the primitive community."[18] That sounds very much like Brooks's idea of himself. Instead, James made himself irrelevant to America by leaving it. Fitzgerald understood the force of allusion—Brooks classified *him* among those expatriates who were deeply ignorant of American issues. The first readers of *The Great Gatsby* would naturally assume that it failed to portray what it should, the national life of America.

The survey of Brooks's career by René Wellek sums him up as a romantic nationalist who wanted literature to mirror a society organic to the point of improbability. In fact, he wanted literature to be "a national voice." Wellek places that school of thought within a larger context: on the continent, after the Great War, "feelings common to the masses of mankind, social problems, became the central topic of most writers. Subjectivism, individualism, anything that savored of decadence was swept away in a great flood of communal experience."[19] Mencken, one of the few who kept up with European criticism, took from Benedetto Croce the opinion that the joyous depiction of national pieties—he called such things "transient platitudes, political, economic and aesthetic"—undermined literary standards. Unfortunately, simply to be independent of such feelings was to be "a bad artist."[20]

Brooks was important enough in the early twenties to be a significant hurdle for Fitzgerald. As editor of the *Freeman,* he was able to enforce a "program for literary America" by patronizing reviewers. They also wrote for other journals—and their "authority was never seriously challenged" until Brooks left his post in 1924.[21] Except, I think, by Fitzgerald. That leaves open the issue of Fitzgerald's compliance to opinion. I don't at all agree with the following: "Writers like Brooks who were active after World War I reacted upon one another, and upon younger writers. In his office at the *Freeman,* Brooks met many of the young intellectuals who were in some degree affected by him—men like Lewis Mumford, Newton Arvin, Walter Lippmann, and Edmund Wilson; and they all, in their different ways, were critical of the money-oriented culture the 1890s gave to the 1920s. It was in this environment of attack upon American materialism that Fitzgerald came of age as a novelist, and it is not surprising that his criticism of American values in *The Great Gatsby* should reflect as much as it does the intellectual life of the twenties."[22]

These critics were intelligently concerned with American issues—but they were not the issues that interested Fitzgerald. He was interested in writing; they were interested in the condition of intellectuals. He was interested in the psychology of wealth; they were interested in its morality. When George

Santayana thought over such differences, he said that moral art pleased only moralists. It was in any case philosophically impossible to locate the point between "*the country's actual condition and its inherent ideal*."[23] Van Wyck Brooks seemed never to have understood Fitzgerald's point—it is derived from both William James and Santayana—that concepts vary from one mind and one moment to another. Finally, as to that issue we honorifically call national debate, John Dewey wrote in 1927 that the "conscious life of opinion and judgment," that is, the subject of our "public matters," was definitively *not* part of "the deeper levels of life" as shown in poetry and novels.[24]

My own interpretation is that *The Great Gatsby* was written against Brooks's "program" of dominating New Grub Street. By 1924 his influence had begun to wane. So had Mencken's. It wouldn't be right to claim that the times were changing—they always are—but there was certainly a new point of equilibrium. Wellek makes the point that modernism had the inestimable advantage over its critics of conforming to social reality. He, too, picks 1924 as the year of modernism's gathering powers.[25] By 1926, when Fitzgerald wrote "How to Waste Material: A Note on My Generation," he had formulated the entire issue. Since the beginning of the decade, books had poured out in ideological profusion on farmers from New England to Nebraska; on the youth culture; on the fate of universities; and on life in New York, Chicago, Washington, Detroit, Indianapolis, Wilmington, and Richmond. There had been, he said, "innumerable novels dealing with American politics, business, society, racial problems, art, literature and moving pictures." In other words, an Arnold Bennett for every five towns, so that "the American scene" had been swamped by social conscience.[26]

Fitzgerald, Hemingway, and other writers reacted strongly to this perception. There was a generational argument, with the modernists abandoning political discourse. Malcolm Cowley, for example, dismissed writers like Randolph Bourne because " 'they' had been rebels: they wanted to change the world, be leaders in the fight for justice and art, help to create a society in which individuals could express themselves." On the other hand, " 'we' were convinced at the time that society could never be changed by an effort of the will." He added, "the writers of our generation . . . did not hope to alter the course of events. . . . Society was either regarded as a sort of self-operating, self-repairing, self-perpetuating machine, or else it was not regarded."[27] As Fitzgerald put the matter in his best-known essay, "it was characteristic of the Jazz Age that it had no interest in politics at all."[28]

~

In that central year 1924, an imaginary dialogue by Lewis Mumford was published in the *American Mercury*. The first speaker ("Charles Adams") is Van Wyck Brooks; one interlocutor ("Edwin O'Malley") is Ernest Boyd, a

Mencken disciple. Boyd has just accused Brooks of being vastly uninterested in literature, alive only to the effect that any given book might produce upon society. Brooks responds, then is followed by Joel Spingarn ("Ernest De Fiori"):

> ADAMS (*unruffled*): You object . . . to the fact that I believe that a community has a permanent self, made up of its best minds and embodied in its literature, as well as the shifting, temporary self which expresses itself in its daily actions and in the opinions of those who control it in the press and on the platform? I can't conceive what function you accord to literature, unless it is to embody that permanent self and make it visible.
>
> DE FIORI: You mustn't confuse an act in the practical world with an act in the spiritual world. The values of literature lie entirely in the spiritual realm: they are independent of the society that has produced a work of art or that may be affected by it. . . . A work of art is good or bad in terms of the author's own world. What was the writer's inner purpose, and how has he accomplished it?"[29]

We recall Fitzgerald telling Brooks that "complicated & ramified" scenes might not fit into a larger conception. There may not be a larger conception. It's been argued that Wilson's *I Thought of Daisy* "was able to capture and put down on paper impressions of the kaleidoscopic motion of life in the Village that also expressed the spirit of the twenties."[30] To be expressive of a decade or even of a moment is harder than it looks. Wilson's next novel, *The Higher Jazz,* has its doubts. Its main character says, "Picasso has been doing in painting very much the same sort of thing that Schoenberg has been doing in music. . . . Distortion is normal to art. It was the photographic nineteenth century in painting that violated the real tradition and made deliberate distortion necessary in order to see the world again the way the artist ought to see it—the way Schoenberg or Picasso sees it. What Julie doesn't understand about Schoenberg is that he's only bringing out certain things—"[31]

The insight has a lot to do with Fitzgerald's practice; and it opens up a set of issues about the limits of expressiveness in music, painting, and writing. There are certainly public values in Fitzgerald—they are in fact vitally important to his work. But he was at this point in his intellectual life equally concerned with the idea of perception. In *The Great Gatsby* he asks not only what America *is* like but what it *looks* like. I will refer briefly to modernist visual art, and then in detail to a part of it that deeply affected both Fitzgerald and Hemingway.

Current art history emphasizes the role of perception in modernism. MoMA 2000, intended to be a three-part cycle of exhibitions by the Museum of Modern Art, concentrates on the components of visual art in the early twentieth century. The first volume of this exhibition to appear, *ModernStarts: People, Places, Things,* argues that the world's only common language is constituted by the "Objects" that surround us. Working from exhibits of still lifes, constructions, and an enormous category of independent forms, *ModernStarts* concludes that "an object in its own right is a significant characteristic of early modernism."[32] Even more, "if one word captures the aspirations of modernism from about 1870 until the Second World War, it is surely object. Firstly in poetry and painting, then in sculpture, music and architecture, the word came to denote an ideal condition of self-sustained, self-generating apartness of the work of art."[33] There is a reason for that. In *Science and the Modern World*—that other great text of 1925—Whitehead wrote that "the ultimate appeal is to naïve experience and that is why I lay such stress on the evidence of poetry." The world is not, he added, completely one of institutions and ideas; it is experienced in terms of colors, sounds, and "objects" in space and time. To see these things is to correct our subjectivity, and see "the experienced world" as it is. Whitehead reminds us—the critics of *The Great Gatsby* were unaware—that "no one idea can in itself be sufficient."[34]

We know that *The Great Gatsby* is about the pursuit of a "grail." And we can be given to understand (as in Walter Crane's 1870 painting *The White Knight*) that a large canvas can be devoted with the most unremitting tedium to the scene of such a quest.[35] But the grail in Fitzgerald shares space. It is there in the sense that Malevich's *Analytical Chart* of 1925 allows for simultaneous occupation of the canvas by scenes and repetitions. We can, I think, compare Fitzgerald's technique to that of Mondrian, whose *Composition* of 1920 has dozens of independent forms. There is the introductory illustration used by the Museum of Modern Art, *The Red Studio* (1911) of Matisse. The whole is composed of entirely different parts, each with its own form and value.[36] They show modernism's hospitality to independent forms. But there are examples close to Fitzgerald, specifically the paintings of Gerald Murphy.

Fitzgerald understood what Murphy had to say about a number of artistic issues. I think that the most important of them were the depiction of space and color and the new sense of mechanical form. What did Fitzgerald see and hear while working on *The Great Gatsby?* Many artists were working around Antibes, including Picasso. They talked about their work and about graphic motifs. They also talked about and reviewed each other's work. Linda Patterson Miller calls Murphy's relationship to writers like Dos Passos, Fitzgerald, and Hemingway a "collective story."[37] And Kenneth Wayne has identified the "four artistic centers" around the Villa America, establishing the connection between a formidable number of artists. The major figures operating between these centers were Picasso, Léger, Man Ray, and Murphy himself. A main theme of this research is interconnection: "A watercolor purportedly of F. Scott Fitzgerald on the beach by Picabia suggests a link between the artist and a key member of the Murphy circle."[38]

Murphy took notes on the objects assembled in his own paintings, calling them contemporary versions of "nature morte."[39] He concentrated on the geometry of specific objects, mechanisms, and surfaces that had been produced by other machines. The phrase about still life may seem out of place until we realize that "the genre of still life became increasingly important in this period, perhaps even rivaling its acclaimed status in seventeenth-century Dutch art. . . . beginning with Paul Cézanne, still life concerned itself with the relationship of . . . proximate objects."[40] That demanded a new and intense concentration on the shape, volume, and relationship of things deep within the frame, the parts that made up the whole. Picasso was at that time working on compositions like *Compotier, mandoline, partition, bouteille.*[41] Like Gerald Murphy, he did stage sets, his own showing isolated parts of the human body, and in one case the female breast "painted red." In 1925, his *L'atelier* imaged a mixture of "sculptured," separated limbs.[42] Murphy himself worked with the ideas of "displacement" and "depersonalization." That meant breaking up the human body into separate forms. The notes to his *Portrait* of 1928 read: "Picture: an eye,—lashes, brow, lids, etc. big scale."[43]

Some of Fitzgerald's objects—by this point we need to call them independent subjects—exist within phrases two words long. And some of them—"her left breast was swinging loose like a flap. . . . The mouth was wide open and ripped at the corners"—reflect the new visualization.[44] *The Great Gatsby* has within it not only the motifs of modernism but its constituents. Its depiction of scenes is forcefully geometric. From Tom Buchanan's eyes to all those "things" floating around in the mind of Myrtle Wilson, Fitzgerald adapts techniques and motifs of visual art.

Mechanization is an overwhelming theme in *Gatsby,* and Murphy, as in his painting *Watch* of 1924–25, was an artist of mechanical detail. His work was known to Fitzgerald, and his standing among painters was envied by him.[45] Murphy's paintings of the early twenties—*Boatdeck, Watch,* and *Razor*—were all kept at the Villa America. He was heavily involved in production and exhibition from 1923 to 1926. Fitzgerald first met him in Paris, in fact, at a point in Murphy's life when ideas about the several arts intersected. This is how Murphy interpreted the moment: "the material at hand was invaluable to anyone the greater part of whose reactions were aesthetic." He was accurate: Zelda Fitzgerald later wrote to Sara and Gerald Murphy that Scott shared their "aesthetic and spiritual purposes of life."[46] William Rubin of the Museum of Modern Art did the 1974 MoMA exhibition *The Paintings of Gerald Murphy* and has this to say of Murphy's intellectual life: "Until his trip to Europe, Murphy had considered painting strictly an art of verisimilitude.... Shortly after arriving in Paris in September of 1921, he saw, quite by chance, some paintings by Picasso, Matisse, Braque and Gris.... His response was intense. 'I was astounded,' Murphy recalled. 'My reaction to the color and form was immediate.'" He tried explicitly to link what he did with American subjects in a painterly language of economy and "stylization." He even had hopes for the development of an American art of "native classicism," that is, the equivalent of what Picasso was doing in Antibes at that time.[47]

Murphy worked within visual limits, his own material being "seen close-up, from an intimate perspective, but . . . viewed impassively."[48] His subjects are connected to his business experience—they are "prosaic objects of American life" that began their own limited lives as "merchandise." This was seen to be an advantage: both Picasso and Léger emphasized the specifically American quality of his material in conversation and in reviews.[49] Both stated that his choice of industrial objects marked him especially as a representative American modernist. Murphy called his own work "*objects* in a world of abstraction."[50] I have said much of this term, and extensive new scholarship has addressed it. Here is what the current (2007) exhibition *Making It New: The Art and Style of Sara and Gerald Murphy* states about his technique: "*Razor*... transfers Gerald's long-standing appreciation of humble objects—in this case, a matchbook, fountain pen, and safety razor—into paint on canvas by elevating the commonplace to high-art status."[51] I think that it would be difficult to approach the text of *The Great Gatsby* without first making such a concession. Murphy's notebook describes a construction using "parts of recognizable household objects," which shows how "the notion of objecthood" became central to his mind.[52] And there is new, sustained appreciation of the point made originally by Picasso that Murphy was "peculiarly American." His compositions depicting "smaller-scaled objects of contemporary life" embody "the world of merchandising and modern advertising."[53] Of course, more was involved: "Cubism was not only a radical form of painting; it also represented a new way of experiencing the world, one tied to the fractured character and staccato pace of modern urban life. Gerald responded immediately to this new kind of picture making, which did not mirror reality but instead shifted, broke apart, and realigned it in unexpected ways. He understood that the Cubist artists were of their time in a profound way, reflecting the uncertain new mechanized age the world had entered."[54] We are forcibly reminded not only of shared imagery between Murphy and Fitzgerald, but of the assumption that visual perception had itself changed.

Here is Meyer Schapiro's overall view of objects in modernism: "Still life, as much as landscape and sometimes more, calls out a response to an implied human presence. Each still-life painting has not only a unique appearance as a whole; the represented objects, in their relation to us, acquire meanings from the desires they satisfy as well as from their analogies and relations to the human body. . . Not a text or an event but some tendency of feeling directing the painterly imagination will determine here a coherent choice of a family of objects. Schapiro refers to the literary "text" often—in this case to Flaubert and Yeats. The object we see is either potentially or fully "a part of human life," he states, in both painting and writing of the twenties.[55] It would appear to be so in Fitzgerald's writing. In a letter of 1935 to Sara Murphy, Fitzgerald described his "theory" of fiction in terms of modernist painting. He had, he admitted, used her often in *Tender Is the Night.* She was present throughout the book but not as a fulfilled character: "in a hundred . . . places I tried to evoke not *you* but the effect that you produce on men—the echoes and reverberations—a poor return for what you have given by your living presence, but nevertheless an artist's (what a word!) sincere attempt to preserve a true fragment rather than a 'portrait' by Mr. Sargent." She was infused into the story in a flash of color or the recollection of a "single part" of her body.[56] William Rubin's MoMA retrospective states that this modernist view of the language of the body came from Klee and Picasso, among others—and also from photography in which documentation gave way to concentration on form. The aim of "recording an appearance" was abandoned, and artists of the twenties avoided "realistic renderings of the human body" as a whole. Instead, "modern pictures are . . . distillations or evocations." We understand the self symbolically through iterations of "personal imagery." Emotions as great as any ever traditionally expressed are here, only in a different way.[57] Rubin notes of Picasso that "the image of Sara Murphy recurs among his drawings."[58] If Picasso and Fitzgerald are doing the same thing with the same subject, it may be worth an intentional fallacy or two.

Is it possible for art to reflect or "express" the large issues that critics of the early twenties so dearly loved? E. H. Gombrich identified the period 1910–25 with the birth of the formal idea of "expression." Specifically, a great revision of art history then took place. It was based on the unproven theory that artists expressed "the spirit of their respective ages." Gombrich believed that this was a theory designed for critics and not for artists. It disposed of the messiness of particularity, allowing any work of art to be read as if it were a direct commentary on its time and place.[59] He returned to this period and to this point in his inaugural lecture at University College, London. Part of the following reads as if it were taken out of Edmund Wilson's imaginary dialogue between Brooks and Fitzgerald: "Mr. Wyndham Lewis may not have been altogether wrong when he blamed the demon of progress on the demon of historicism. The art historian who sees the styles of the past merely as an expression of the age, the race or the class-situation, will torment the living artist with the empty demand that he should go and do likewise and express the essence and spirit of his time, race, class or, worst of all, of the self. The more we exorcize those spirits which still haunt the history of art, the more we learn to look at the individual and particular work of art."[60] In yet a third argument, Gombrich took this position: "No one would deny that there is a genuine problem hidden here. There is such a thing as a mental climate, a pervading attitude in periods or societies, and art and artists are bound to be responsive to certain shifts in dominant values." There is, however, no point in believing uncritically in "nations, races, classes or periods as unified psychological entities."[61] All these categories are subject to (infinite) interpretation. I think that this goes back to Whitehead's distinction between the world we experience, that is *there*, and the world of ideas and institutions that we construct to account for it—although they don't succeed.

Lionel Trilling's essay on Fitzgerald in *The Liberal Imagination* is broadly in agreement with Gombrich's ideas. According to Trilling, *The Great Gatsby* is certainly about the American Dream; and we are intended to see the nation in the individual. But, because the novel is about a given moment as well as about a grand conception, it is not easily universalized. Trilling defines the thematic American quality of the novel in these terms: immense national power haunted by envisioned romance. However, he does not develop the assertion, and this part of the essay is a rarely opaque moment in his text. At this point, he does exactly what Gombrich does (and what Azar Nafisi was later to do), moving from the tortured issue of expressive meaning to the simpler ground of perception and depiction.[62] All three writers state that the final judgment on art is how a *scene* proceeds from brush stroke or word.[63]

In one of the best essays on the problem of representation in Fitzgerald, Malcolm Bradbury wrote that his characters are "propelled by history and society into expressive action." However, Fitzgerald never unites history and character because both are continually in process. So, there can never be more than "limited meanings" to look for.[64] That resonates with Fitzgerald's own view of the relationship of context to experience. I don't think he wrote a more important critical line than the one in the letter to Max Perkins about intellectual nostalgia: the "*stubborn seeking for the static in a world that for al-*

most a hundred years has simply not been static." Even Gatsby does not believe in that—although it is a cherished ideal of Tom Buchanan, patron of civilization and the arts.

The first readers of *The Great Gatsby* wanted American novels to criticize the world in being. Major critics, including Brooks, Mencken, and even Edmund Wilson, did not believe that Fitzgerald had provided a synthetic view of America. However, Walter Lippmann had already provided an argument against such thought in 1922: "in the great blooming, buzzing confusion of the outer world we pick out *what our culture has already defined for us,* and we tend to perceive that which we have picked out in the form stereotyped for us by our culture."[65] The evidence is that Fitzgerald was broadly in agreement. He did not say that he placed his characters within a social structure or that he had conceptualized his subject. He did say that he placed his characters within "a moment in time and space."[66] There were contingent issues: Brooks wanted literature to connect itself to the idealized world of the past—a world that Fitzgerald thought may never have existed. Mencken thought that *The Great Gatsby* was morally trivial. Wilson's editor thinks that he tried to have characters of *The Higher Jazz* illustrate or "express" the "self-destructive 1920s in their disordered private lives."[67] He could not achieve that, and the novel remained unpublished for years. When Wilson went over his other novel about the twenties, *I Thought of Daisy,* he acknowledged that it could not compare with *The Great Gatsby.* He had described the feelings and ideas of some intellectuals about some issues but could not compete with Fitzgerald's drama, language, and character.[68] Wilson got *The Shores of Light* and *The Twenties* out of his formulation. Mencken got Dreiser and Sinclair Lewis. Brooks got *The Ordeal of Mark Twain.* These are not small things—but they never sank a harpoon into Leviathan.

3
Fitzgerald's Autobiographies

"I'll tell you God's truth," Gatsby says to Nick Carraway, and begins a sequence of autobiographical lies.[1] The statement comes just after Gatsby's assurance that Nick will understand the difference between his life and "stories you hear" about it. But in Fitzgerald, stories and lives are not separated. Revelation and recollection in Fitzgerald combine fact and fiction. The line assigned to Gatsby has a life of its own, and there are two early versions of it in "Myra Meets His Family" (1920). A rich boy, Knowleton Whitney, says earnestly that he has "something . . . to tell" Myra about his family before adding her to it. But he has rented fake ancestral portraits—and even a set of stage parents—in order to discourage her attempt to marry him. Overcome temporarily by virtue, he later says, "I'm going to tell you the whole story."[2] Is it worth hearing? Myra understands the connection of "tell" and "story" to truth; and she does not want to spend the rest of her life listening to permutations of that phrase. So she hires her own family—a cousin conveniently in orders—and goes through a faked marriage ceremony. And then she leaves Whitney permanently in a compartment of the Broadway Limited, thinking over the consequences of authorship.

Fitzgerald's protagonists have more than situational uses for exaggerations, inventions, and downright lies about their own identities. Self-formulation was a national subject, investigated by William James in *The Principles of Psychology.* This work contained more analysis of national style and character than its title might suggest. The Modern Library edition of 1925 divided it into sections called "The Self," "The American Scene," and "The Individual and Society." James identified "the social self" in America in terms of the worrisome guises it needed to adopt: "a division of the man into several selves; and this may be a discordant splitting." Given Fitzgerald's great subject, one of James's conclusions is especially telling: our own selves are at their most divergent when dealing with "the mind of the person one is in love with."[3] However, this text was not limited to the small theatrics of everyday life. The editor of the Modern Library edition, Horace M. Kallen, pointed out that James's ideas of fragmented individuality applied specifically to the new conditions of American life in the twenties. Kallen was anxious to provide the moment with its meaning, and he used James to argue that a new kind of individualism had arrived. It made anything seem possible; instead of a single cosmic system governing all, there were apartness, change, continual movement, new "beginnings" and unforeseen "endings." Modern life had become, he wrote, a matter of "discontinuities," and the very idea of "onenesses" disappeared.[4] That last is a useful extrapolation, referring, I think, to *A Pluralistic Universe* (1909), in which James had written that after major intellectual change arrives, "*all* the old identities at last give out."[5]

George Santayana had this Jamesian text in mind. He wrote in 1920 that "never was the human mind master of so many facts and sure of so few principles." Santayana unhappily mentions the "new realism" in America that failed to apply facts to principles, and hence failed at the same time to interpret our national life.[6] No one seemed to know exactly who he was, only what he was doing and what he had been. Fitzgerald was not alone in his conception of the fluidity of national character. He puts the issue in dramatic form in "Head and Shoulders." Here is Horace Tarbox in 1920, thinking over his own confused life:

> He began to turn over in his mind his own half-forgotten dreams.
>
> He had meant to write a series of books, to popularize the new realism as Schopenhauer had popularized pessimism and William James pragmatism.
>
> But life hadn't come that way. . . . Life took hold of people and forced them into flying rings.
>
> "And it's still me," he said aloud in wonder as he lay awake in the darkness.[7]

This and other Fitzgerald stories concern "identities" as part of the American context.

Fitzgerald uses the inherently ambiguous forms of biography and autobiography to correspond with American lives. Richard Ellmann has written of biography that it conducts experiments "comparable to those of the novel and poem. It cannot be so mobile as those forms because it is associated with history, and must retain a chronological pattern, though not necessarily a simple one."[8] We recall that *The Great Gatsby* has biographies of Tom and

Daisy by Nick, of Jimmy Gatz by his father, of Daisy by Jordan. It has autobiographies by Nick, Jordan, Daisy, Myrtle Wilson, and even Mrs. McKee. The stories repeatedly use both genres with the same degree of creative inexactitude. Patricia Meyer Spacks has written of autobiography that it is never "honest." The form "involves necessary fictions, artifices of self-exposure, masks through which alone the self can be known. Autobiographers realized this fact before critics did; thus Goethe, in conversation with Eckermann . . . remarked, speaking of his own autobiography, 'A fact of our life has validity not by its being true, but rather by its being significant.' "[9]

All writers of life stories deal with an argument established by Locke and later reasserted by William James: "personal identity" is linked to "preservation of memory."[10] The connection is affected by the reliability of memory and, as Goethe implied, by our choice of memories. One of the most searching essays on this subject is by Wallace Fowlie: "As the events in an autobiography form a pattern, it may appear to be prose fiction. At least it uses all the devices a novel does: characters and the chronicle of a family, maxims and lyric passages, confessions and narrative. . . . The use of memory, indispensable to autobiography, is a recycling of memories, both conscious and subconscious aspects of living, by means of which a life story may be transformed into a personal myth. Images persistently return in this recycling, and typical scenes or episodes return. These images and patterns reveal the identity of the writer, to himself first, and then to a reader."[11] In "Early Success," Fitzgerald wrote that he became conscious of his professionalism only when he understood the imposition of form on experience: "a sort of stitching together of your whole life into a pattern of work."[12] And he depended on the recycling of images and ideas in those closely related genres, fiction and nonfiction.

Paul Fussell has this to say about the connection: "the problem for any biographer of an imaginative writer is that writers pursue their mystery by telling great resounding inventions, or lies. The more important of these are called novels, plays and poems; the less important, letters, prefaces, memoirs, journals, and diaries, and we can add essays and travel books as well."[13] In a reflective moment, Fitzgerald reached a similar conclusion. He described to his daughter "a pathological liar in police court" who rearranged facts in order to provide an alibi. In another life, he thought, she "might have been a great creator of fiction."[14] There is a certain amount of self-deprecation here and free-floating wit, but the idea rests on its own feet.

Fitzgerald's stories of self-creation have an underlying structure of interrogation. Action proceeds from assertions about identity that require answers. In order to argue their identities, Fitzgerald's characters need to choose an aspect of their selves to reveal. That is inherently perilous, as when Ailie Calhoun in "The Last of the Belles" guesses "wrong" about the way society will be after the Great War. In the postscript to her story, the model of the belle has been replaced by that of the flapper, so that her position becomes untenable. There is another barrier to the claims of identity, protagonists having to account not only for their invented selves but for their history. We begin with inquiry, proceed through choice, skirt the dangers of fact, and finally convert "story" into "life." For a sense of how such patterns work we might turn to Jasper Johns, who recently reviewed his own production: "I can see in my work things other people might not see—limitations, repetitions, states of mind."[15]

~

Curtis Carlyle in "The Offshore Pirate" (1920) restates a familiar phrase: "I've got to tell you the—the truth." But his story takes the inherently suspect form of autobiography. The opening—he "began life as a poor kid in a Tennessee town" (79)—follows a literary pattern antedating Horatio Alger. Curtis goes from the provinces to New York—and from poverty to wealth. However, he has a discerning audience. Ardita Farnum is iconoclastic and does not want to hear yet one more version of rising in America. So the story is modernized, becoming a contemporary portrait of the artist as a young man. The essential part of this story occurs *after* success, which also is generic. His theme, endlessly replayed by the entertainment industry, takes the form of a rigid sequence: after popularity comes success; after success comes disillusion; and after disillusion comes pathos. But in this story, after pathos comes the loss of identity. That is because it contains more than one autobiography. Curtis Carlyle fears becoming "a sort of sublimated chorus man" (80)—and Alec McKaig's diaries of 1920–21 state that Fitzgerald thought that he might succeed in New York only "by becoming another Booth Tarkington, which meant selling out for popularity."[16] And we recognize another kind of narrative about America as the twenties begin. That "story" is shaped around certain issues.

Life stories require a philosophy as well as a history. Curtis decides to account for the false relationship between patrons and performers. I think he does so because it was a subject on Fitzgerald's mind. He was soon to state (1921) that in the modern world, as ever, "art follows begging after money."[17] Curtis is nothing if not adaptive, and he cites a theory about democracy in America that actually comes from *Democracy in America.* A key chapter in Tocqueville, "Of Individualism in Democracies," had observed that democracies promote selfishness and worship money. Being classless, they have no class.[18] The countervailing idea of aristocracy appeals to Curtis, who mentions it to Ardita. We know that it appealed to Fitzgerald because he acknowledged his debt to the cultural theories of H. L. Mencken in which it is embedded.

From 1917 on, Mencken wrote voluminous arguments on the contrast between democratic and aristocratic culture. One of his best-known essays, "The Sahara of the Bozart," combines an attack on southern culture with arguments defining "a genuine aristocracy" of styles and ideas.[19] Along with "American Culture," that essay had been reprinted in *Prejudices: Second Series,* a collection reviewed by Fitzgerald in 1921.[20] A later essay, "Politics," appeared in Harold E. Stearns's *Civilization in the United States* (1922). There, Mencken described the House of Representatives as a collection of political hacks and religious fakirs whose debates now and then reached as high as McGuffey's Fifth Reader. It was not enough that they could be bought; nor that they were Prohibitionists. The provinces still dominated the nation through the sequential election of men "devoid of any contact with what passes for culture."[21] Mencken's view of culture in democracy echoed Tocqueville—and also many writers of the twenties. Here, for example, is Van Wyck Brooks: "Mencken . . . urges that the only hope of a change for the better lies in the development of a native aristocracy that will stand between the writer and the public, supporting him, appreciating him, forming as it were a *cordon sanitaire* between the individual and the mob. That no change can come without the development of an aristocracy of some sort, some nucleus of the more gifted, energetic and determined, one can hardly doubt."[22] It was a very hazy notion because of the confusion between culture and politics. The argument did not survive Walter Lippmann's analysis of the way that ideas functioned in a democracy:

> The old aristocracies which Mr. Mencken admires did not delude themselves with any nonsense about liberty. They reserved what liberty there was for a privileged elite, knowing perfectly well that if you granted liberty to every one you would have sooner or later everything that Mr. Mencken deplores. But he seems to think that you can have a privileged, ordered, aristocratic society with complete liberty of speech. That is as thorough-going a piece of Utopian sentimentalism as anything could be. You might as well proclaim yourself a Roman Catholic and then ask that excerpts from the *American Mercury* and the works of Charles Darwin be read from the altar on the first Sunday of each month. If Mr. Mencken really wishes an aristocracy he will have to give up liberty as he understands it; and if he wishes liberty he will have to resign himself to hearing *homo boobiens* speak his mind."[23]

Fitzgerald's work of the twenties moved away from Mencken and toward the view that status and success were empirically determined. My sense of it is that Fitzgerald is a more reliable guide to American economics than his idealistic mentors, and that includes Edmund Wilson, who also longed for restrictions on free enterprise. Fitzgerald understood two important points: how wealth was actually made, and how it ennobles itself. As for "aristocracy," his rich boys have nothing *inherent* in them, only the power of money. In Fitzgerald social class is dynamic. James R. Mellow's biography dismisses his "view of the aristocrat as being the hard-line capitalist who summered at Newport or Bar Harbor and sent his sons to Princeton and Yale."[24] But Fitzgerald was not confused about the composition of our new upper class. His diagnosis has been borne out by a recent business history of the decade of the twenties: "The men who dominated the Exchange were pale imitations of the Morgan mold. They came largely from Yankee stock, had gone to the best New England schools, where they majored in sports and making the right connections, were more shrewd than bright, thrived on urban club life, and tended to be snobs despite their general ignorance of art, literature, music, history, and world affairs. Their overriding interests, which they made no attempt to disguise, were making money and climbing the social ladder."[25] The above—real-world economics—refers to the year 1920.

~

It can reasonably be said that "The Offshore Pirate" is unbelievable, but not that it is trivial. Subjects that it raises will persist in Fitzgerald's work. Principal among them is the extraordinary amount of effort that goes into a convincing autobiography. Fitzgerald's characters from Ailie Calhoun to Jimmy Gatz struggle with the *story* of their own lives. The task of autobiography, like that of fiction, defeats the author. Curtis Carlyle's "autobiography" becomes more centrifugal as he tries to deal not only with the penalties of success but *with the momentum of his own authorial sequence.* We are left with certain insights into the created self: the most necessary lies concern our identity; and "family," which is after all the origin of self, is one of the least trustworthy nouns in America.

Two stories of 1922 are composed of doubts about the familial or original self. They connect this subject with American democracy. "The Curious Case of Benjamin Button" is, I think, less of a fantasy than "The Offshore Pirate." Only chronology is reversed: husbands grow away from their wives, fathers misunderstand their sons, sons are ashamed of their fathers, money matters quite a lot more than values. One subject of this story is the relationship of fathers and sons. Another is middle-class imagination. "Family" is an unstable word here, as it is in "The Offshore Pirate" and in *The Great Gatsby.*

Benjamin Button's family is connected to Yale and also to what Fitzgerald calls the "peerage" of the Confederacy. Because the members of his family are such ciphers, they weaken the legitimacy of institutions that depend on them. Even the term *family* is a dissolvent, although it pretends otherwise. Throughout this story the idea of individual identity is poised against a kind of social nominalism.

Is that a far-fetched observation? Patricia Meyer Spacks has this to say about subjective reality: "Our experience of life, obviously, does not proceed by an orderly sequence of clearly distinguished stages. On a particular day we may suddenly realize that we are, or are considered by others, old, or middle-aged, or even adolescent, but no sounding trumpets mark the transition."[26] Or, as our hero puts it, "I can't tell you *exactly* who I am" (162). The last days of Benjamin Button's life story—with "no troublesome memories" (180)—were to be revived in 1936: "So there was not an 'I' any more—not a basis on which I could organize my self-respect—save my limitless capacity for toil that it seemed I possessed no more. It was strange to have no self—to be like a little boy left alone in a big house, who knew that now he could do anything he wanted to do, but found that there was nothing that he wanted to do—"[27] The line "It was strange to have no self" is an important one in the period from James to Freud. When James wrote about "character" he emphasized its location in identity: "there is a voice inside which speaks and says: '*This* is the real me!' We compare that with a character who says that he can't 'tell you *exactly* who I am.'" James, like Fitzgerald in his later essay, developed the point: take away self-recognition and you remove "the deepest principle of all active and theoretic determination." If the self is uncertain, the world cannot be experienced. James's subject was depression, leading from loss of self to "genuine thoughts, and genuine acts, of suicide, spiritual and social."[28]

This is not an admired story. But Fitzgerald's lesser stories have components that matter more than the whole. Recurrent images and ideas unify separated works: Fitzgerald's southern stories can be seen in the light of his businesslike assessment of *Gone with the Wind.* The jejune idea of "aristocracy" in "The Offshore Pirate" breaks out of its chrysalis in "Winter Dreams." Benjamin Button has more than one life and reappears in *The Crack-up.* One of the great clichés of magazine culture, the southern belle, becomes the powerful and mysterious *figura* of American desire in *The Great Gatsby.*

"Winter Dreams," that superb story of 1922, asks, "Who are you, anyhow?" In the light of James's concentration on our *choice* of selves, this remark has considerable depth.[29] Even more so, I think, when we compare it to the circulation of Freud's ideas in *The Ego and the Id* (1923). Freud made the point that identity was accumulative. "An individual's first and most important identification" was with his father. Thereafter, one hopes, we assimilated ideas about "a higher nature in man." After that came the myriad transformations of early ideals by experience.[30] Our social desire is to create ideal selves—but the process can never be painless. In fact, it may not be successful. "What is repressed in mental life" may be a very great loss for personality—an outcome bound to shock the psychoanalytically innocent.[31] In this particular story, Fitzgerald recognizes that there is more than one story to tell *or to withhold:*

> For a moment Dexter hesitated. There were two versions of his life that he could tell. There was Dillard and his caddying and his struggle through college, or—
>
> "I'm nobody," he announced.[32]

One of the most cutting things about this passage is Dexter Green's use of the same term for himself—"nobody"—that Tom Buchanan contemptuously applies to Jay Gatsby. He has internalized that particular notion of identity, although it may not be the most important issue raised by his decision.

Dexter is full of hesitations about how much of himself he can reveal, how much he can add, how much of himself he needs to abandon. The assumptions are profoundly American because the decision is based on choice. That is to say, we approach the project of our own identities as if they were like anything else encountered in the progressive movement of social life. They change as we want them to change. But there is an exceptionally interesting passage in Malcolm Cowley about the way change turns into constraint. Cowley is thinking about one of the great Hemingway problems, how he turned himself into a persona for the marketplace. Were psychic costs incurred when Hemingway went from being a writer to a public figure and culture hero? Cowley refers to Jung, who wrote that "A man cannot get rid of himself in favor of an artificial personality without punishment. Even the attempt to do so brings on, in all ordinary cases, unconscious reactions."[33] As Cowley saw the issue, Hemingway's later life, full of symbolic recriminations, doubts, and even self-punishments, was a response to his decision to remake himself. These occurred *after* attaining his goals. The long reflection on life that ends "Winter Dreams" is about a loss of self never imagined by the ideology of success.[34] Fitzgerald returned to the theme in his essay "Early Success" in 1937. He wrote (it is part of his own autobiography) that "the dream had been early realized and the realization carried with it a certain bonus and a certain burden. Premature success gives one an almost mystical conception of destiny as opposed to will power." He wrote also that one could fall into "delusions" if the impersonal movement of history were disregarded.[35] I touch this point briefly but it is important enough for much reconsideration.

Dexter's life takes the form of (literally) patterned, controlled imitation: "He had known who were the best tailors in America, and the best tailor in America had made him the suit he wore this evening. He had acquired that particular reserve peculiar to his university, that set it off from other universities. He recognized the value to him of such a mannerism and he had adopted it. . . . His mother's name had been Krimslich. She was a Bohemian of the peasant class and she had talked broken English to the end of her days. Her son must keep to the set patterns."[36] H. L. Mencken had just provided a script for such new men, writing in "American Culture" that success is never enough for a man to enter our national "aristocracy" of wealth. "He must exhibit exactly the right social habits, appetites and prejudices, public and private. He must harbor exactly the right enthusiasms . . . [and] stick to the right haberdashery."[37] Fitzgerald adapted Mencken's script—this is what the bourgeois aristocracy looks like from the outside:

> And so while he waited for her to appear he peopled the soft deep summer room and the sun porch that opened from it with the men who had already loved Judy Jones. He knew the sort of men they were—the men who when he first went to college had entered from the great prep-schools with graceful clothes and the deep tan of healthy summer, who did nothing or anything with the same debonair ease.
>
> Dexter had seen that, in one sense, he was better than these men. He was newer and stronger. Yet in acknowledging to himself that he wished his children to be like them he was admitting that he was but the rough, strong stuff from which this graceful aristocracy eternally sprang.[38]

In one of his last pieces, Fitzgerald returned to the language of this passage. He states in 1939 that he has been thinking of the generation of 1800, especially of Daniel Webster and Andrew Jackson. They made their way to power *without* being to the mannerism born. These self-made men were "rougher" and more "strongly individual" than those they replaced.[39] They are part of a historical process. When we read the later passage we see in the earlier one contempt—and also memories of H. G. Wells, whose eloi were graceful and food for morlocks.

Dexter understands that self-invention can go only so far, and he is remarkably firm about avoiding polarities. There is always the temptation to become what one envies, to impersonate the subject.[40] However, there is very little "self-pity and ostentation" in this literal view of social history.[41] One other psychological problem exists—Fitzgerald later called it being "haunted always by my other life."[42] But Dexter navigates between these things. His language is dispassionate, even cold-blooded, and completely accurate. In *The American Language,* Mencken cited Salvador de Madariaga (1928) in praise of "those English monosyllables" that stayed so close to the verbal fact: "one is tempted to think English words are the right and proper names which acts are meant to have, and all other words are pitiable failures."[43] They are, so to speak, final definitions. In Fitzgerald, starkly reductive language takes on a particular role. It gives believability. Terms like *soft, deep, new,* and *strong* have no modulations. They are what they are and there is no arguing with them. The "glacial impersonality" that Paul Rosenfeld saw in Fitzgerald's prose consists, I think, of his poising will against necessity.[44] If we concentrate on the intense presence of romantic feeling in Fitzgerald we may not be aware of the hard, logical deposit under those feelings.

The terms *tell, truth,* and *story* are never really abandoned. The narrator of "The Last of the Belles" says this about Ailie Calhoun's *apologia pro vita sua:* "it's true. . . . She told me herself" (453). It is 1929, and the locution has become familiar to Fitzgerald's readers. This story multiplies the odds because Ailie needs different stories for different listeners. The narrator calls her a "chameleon" (461); she has recently been described as "a good imitation of a kind of figment of the Southern imagination."[45] That last differs from the text. Girls like her make up "a Northern man's dream of the South" (460). Ailie's primary audience comes from above the Mason-Dixon line, men like Earl Schoen who see her in terms of sentimental movies and magazine stories. There is a secondary audience of southern men with local knowledge. Next are skeptical Tarleton friends who know most of the truth but say little about it. And there are a few, including the narrator, who can say that they "recognized her" (451) empirically. Her character seems to be immorally various—although James had stated that "properly speaking, *a man has as many social selves as there are individuals who recognize him* and carry an image of him in their mind. . . . he has as many different social selves as there are distinct *groups* of persons about whose opinion he cares."[46]

The issue is worked out dramatically when the bewitched Earl Schoen—who has been wallowing around Ailie in the pool—deserts Kitty Preston. Kitty reminds Ailie about grand theft, Ailie reminds Kitty that possession is nine-tenths of the law. The great point, though, is that Ailie has three kinds of conversation at the same time: she acts like a belle to Earl, like a critic to the narrator, and like a plantocrat to Kitty. The episode ends with her asserting a superbly manufactured standard of "breeding" against "commonness." If there really is a Jamesian hierarchy of available selves, then we pick the ones we need. Fitzgerald observes in this story that "the traditional way of behaving" is an assumption in every sense of the term (451).

Fitzgerald's stories about new selves are also about new social (and philosophical) realities. No matter how romantic, his protagonists have to place their sense of self within history. Dexter Green of "Winter Dreams" understands that class relations have changed, allowing mobility through money. He knows also that there are two schemes of time governing him: the moment of his desire, and the immense span—his whole life, really—between that desire and its fulfillment. Curtis Carlyle of "The Offshore Pirate" understands that class values have changed from high-culture themes of restraint to expressive freedom. The discussion of "entertainment" alone in this story underlines its temporal fluidity. Fitzgerald is assiduous about movies, music, and magazines because, far from being imaginative escapes from reality, they compose the new sense of reality itself. By knowing that, Curtis reaches Ardita. The social world of "The Last of the Belles" begins with the impossible assumption that there has been no change in social life. Ailie Calhoun represents "a suggested background of devoted fathers, brothers and admirers stretching back into the South's heroic age" (450). That subject recurred a decade later when Fitzgerald advised David Selznick to show "a background seen or remembered" in the opening of *Gone with the Wind.* In order to show "disappointed love," which he took to be the subject of the film, the script needed first of all to proceed from some concrete facts. It needed to show a genuine *stasis* in which "happiness" had been experienced and from which history had departed.[47] Is there such a "background" in this story? The movie eventually found one—the opening scenes are among the best in the film—but "The Last of the Belles" takes its power from the absence of a real past.

Ailie Calhoun is an unwilling part of the "newer South" (460), and her story registers social change from the First World War to the early twenties. In other words, she has to invent both self and history. As was his way, Fitzgerald kept the cultural issues in mind. His late essay "My Generation" goes over the same period. It revives the story's theme and terminology about "a generation which was doomed to have no successors" (461). For *both* North and South, the old America "passed away somewhere between 1910 and 1920; and the fact gives my generation its uniqueness—we are at once pre-war and post-war. We were well grown in the tense spring of 1917, but for the most part not married and settled. . . . So we inherited two worlds—the one of hope to which we had been bred, the one of disillusion which we had discovered early for ourselves. And that first world was growing as remote as another country."[48] The passage is interesting in its own right and, I think, important for its context. Fitzgerald was able to do exactly what his critics would in 1925 accuse him of failing to do, account for social reality. However, he did not depict America in categorical terms like "Youth" or "Business." In fact, he wrote in very much the same way that John Dewey did in 1930, a year after this story. Dewey's essay "The Lost Individual" is about the same subject. At the end of the twenties there were, he wrote, "conspicuous signs of the disintegration of individuality due to failure to reconstruct the self so as to meet the realities of present social life." He seems to validate Fitzgerald's accuracy and he certainly takes the same point of view: "Instances of the flux in which individuals are loosened from the ties that once gave order and support to their lives are glaring. . . . The beliefs and ideals that are uppermost in their consciousness are not relevant to the society in which they outwardly act and which constantly reacts upon them. Their conscious ideas and standards are inherited from an age that has passed away; their minds . . . are at odds with actual conditions. This profound split is the cause of distraction and bewilderment."[49] Both are concerned with the same "generation," but reading Fitzgerald is like reading Dewey in better prose. There are deep issues in small narratives: Horace Tarbox wakes up to the realization that his old standards are useless; while Ailie Calhoun tries hopelessly to adapt to those new "actual conditions" of social life. That is to say little of Nick Carraway's state of mind.

Fitzgerald's "disillusion" and also Dewey's "bewilderment" apply to the story. Ailie is part of a cast of characters—Sally Carrol Happer in "The Ice Palace," Jim Powell in "Dice, Brassknuckles & Guitar," Daisy Fay and Jordan Baker in *The Great Gatsby*—who move from South to North. Jordan and Daisy exchange innocence for sophistication; Sally Carrol Happer tries to live the *vita activa;* and even Jelly-beans want to change their lives instead of inhabiting them. The narrator wants to solve his unhappiness by finding permanence in the South while Ailie, after seeing Yale and New York, has "turned her eyes North" (451). Her particular problem is alluded to by the essay; it is the loss of belief in that part of the self that depends on the past. The narrator persists while she is involved with more important issues, chief among them holding her "self" together when there is, so to speak, no documentary evidence for its existence. Things are even more fluid than they seem. This story appeared as the thirties were about to begin, and Ruth Prigozy has pointed out that the flapper's life of "dancing, drinking, and flirting" is necessarily about to change. Having displaced the belle, it will give way in fiction and in movies to "finding a place" in a new and more earnest world.[50]

There is one other point, and it refers directly to writing. When Earl

Schoen—who is pretty far down the chain of being—says that "this aristocrat stuff is all right if you got the money for it" (459), he speaks not only for himself but for his reeducated author. It is the most perceptive line of literary criticism in the story, reminding us of Marjorie's dismissal of Louisa May Alcott in "Bernice Bobs Her Hair." The line is a farewell to the fantasies of Ruth Draper and Marse Chan—and also to those of H. L. Mencken and Van Wyck Brooks.

4
Hemingway

Thinking about Cézanne

In a classic study, Emily Stipes Watts pointed out that Hemingway turned to Cézanne "for techniques of describing landscapes" and was able to "transpose" those techniques "into verbal descriptions."[1] Hemingway alluded to the visual arts over four decades, especially to the landscapes of Paul Cézanne and postimpressionism. In 1922, he described his daily walk in Paris through the Luxembourg Gardens to the Musée where he repeatedly saw works of Cézanne and Monet, "thinking inside himself that they had done with paint and canvas what he had been striving to do with words all morning in his room at the old hotel."[2] In 1924, he wrote to Gertrude Stein about "trying to do the country like Cézanne and having a hell of a time and sometimes getting it a little bit."[3] In 1934, he said that true reporting was as hard as "painting a Cézanne."[4] And in 1949, in an interview with Lillian Ross, Hemingway talked at length about the connection between writing and painting. Part of this long interview took place at the Metropolitan Museum of Art: "After we reached the Cézannes and Degas and the other Impressionists, Hemingway became more and more excited, and discoursed on what each artist could do and how and what he had learned from each . . . Hemingway spent several minutes looking at Cézanne's 'Rocks—Forest of Fontainbleau.' 'This is what we try to do in writing, this and this, and the woods, and the rocks we have to climb over,' he said. 'Cézanne is my painter, after the early painters. . . . I can make a landscape like Mr. Paul Cézanne. I learned how to make a landscape from Mr. Paul Cézanne by walking through the Luxembourg Museum a thousand times.' "[5] Hemingway had much to say about modernist painting in *A Moveable Feast,* which was finished in 1960. His allusions are not specific and he does not describe his own translation of painterly technique. Some questions necessarily follow, beginning with what he meant by "landscape." That is, after all, not a simple concept—in his lifetime, it changed radically more than once. What was being said about landscape while he was thinking about it? What technical things did he do with the ideas that he absorbed? His own explanation in *A Moveable Feast* is enigmatic: "I went there nearly every day for the Cézannes and to see the Manets and the Monets and the other Impressionists. . . . I was learning something from the painting of Cézanne that made writing simple true sentences far from enough to make the stories have the dimensions that I was trying to put in them. I was learning very much from him but I was not articulate enough to explain it to anyone. Besides it was a secret."[6] More, one imagines, a mystery, which, according to the *Oxford English Dictionary,* is both a secret and also a "highly technical operation in a trade or art."

There are sources for Hemingway's ideas about painting. Gertrude Stein was his mentor for modern art in the early twenties.[7] We know that her ideas stayed in his mind for a long time.[8] However, she was by no means the first to believe that Cézanne had redefined modernism. A considerable time before she passed on her ideas to Hemingway, Roger Fry had set about his enterprise of making Cézanne the benchmark of twentieth-century style for the visual and other arts. In 1910, three years before the Armory Show, he put on the monumental Manet and the Post-Impressionists in London with its twenty-one Cézannes and also works by Gauguin, van Gogh, Seurat, Matisse, and Picasso. In 1912, at the second postimpressionist show, Cézanne "was represented by eleven works only, but he was the only nineteenth-century man in the show, dominating, as it were, a host of living men, some of them still young, and including Matisse and Picasso, as well as Vlaminck, Derain, Braque, Friesz, and Bonnard."[9] From the Armory Show until the end of the Great War there was, according to John Rewald, "an avalanche of writing" about Cézanne—much of it ferociously hostile. Rewald states that history has a splendid sense of humor, and the opposition is now in a malebolge of its own making.[10] The tide turned with Roger Fry's defining work on Cézanne in 1927. Paul Rosenberg and Lionello Venturi did the great catalogue for their time in 1936. Virginia Woolf redefined the importance of both Cézanne and Fry in her critical biography of the latter in 1940. Kenneth Clark's *Landscape into Art* appeared in 1949; by the early fifties there were important studies of art in general and of Cézanne in particular by Herbert Read, André Malraux, and Meyer Schapiro. A significant amount of commentary covered the connection of painting to writing (and of painters to writers) in Hemingway's lifetime.

In the early part of the twentieth century, critics, reviewers, and publishers often treated new painters and new writers as common enemies. Here is Max Perkins explaining to Hemingway why the manuscript of *A Farewell to Arms* was meeting resistance from editors at Scribner's: "There was a great deal of hostility to 'The Sun.' It was routed and driven off the field by the book's qualities, and the adherence which they won. The hostility was very largely that which any new thing in art must meet, simply because it is disturbing. It shows life in a different aspect, and people are more comfortable when they have got it all conventionalized. . . . It was the same failure to be understood that a wholly new painter meets."[11] Perkins invokes one of the great themes of modernism, the appropriate punishment for making it new—and he also assumes that painting and writing are naturally comparative.

Both implicit meanings bulk large in Cézanne criticism. Before Hemingway wrote about his own imitation of painting by writing, it had been assumed that Cézanne had been trying to imitate writing by painting. A special kind of writing was involved: he and Emile Zola were boyhood friends, each with enormous artistic ambitions. They spent a great deal of time together exploring the terrain around Aix and discussing their perceptions. Roger Fry thought that they both intended not only to describe in different mediums the "sunburnt rocks and the aromatic scrub and the ilex groves" but to reinterpret "landscape" as a set of ideas.[12] In fact, Cézanne became the subject of a Zola novel (*L'oeuvre*) about problems of artistic creation; while "some of the narrative paintings may have been intended as illustrations" of Zola's novels."[13] Although Zola took the early lead, Cézanne left him well behind. Trying, reluctantly, to account for Cézanne's reputation among painters, James G. Huneker judged him to be a kind of unfinished realist with ideological connections to Zola: "he detests design, prearranged composition. . . . He paints what he sees without flattery, without flinching from any ugliness." Huneker raised another important point: there is no "sermon" in his landscape.[14] On a more informed level, Kenneth Clark's *Landscape into Art* adds to the Zola comparison some ideas about discipline, design, and intent. Clark thought that Cézanne's *Les quais* . . . is a well-designed picture, with Cézanne's usual sense of pattern, but the important thing about it is its realism—and I use that word in the sense in which it was used by Cézanne's boyhood friend, Émile Zola." Over a twenty-year period, according to Clark, Cézanne learned to rely not on sentiment but sight.[15] This opinion was published the same year as the Ross interview with Hemingway. Clark emphasized something that we can see is common to Cézanne and Hemingway: landscape (as in *The Sun Also Rises*) is pitilessly free of affect. Not the least of Clark's points is the constant exertion of discipline displayed by reworking the subject. When Hemingway spoke to Ross on the connection between painting and writing—especially the connection between himself and Cézanne—he was stating a fact. His conception was already in the mainstream of modern art history.

A recent study of Cézanne discusses his "narration" and the various forms that it takes. His landscape painting consciously became a way of ordering human sensibility. Landscape was not entirely a matter of aesthetics. It allowed the reduction of the human world to a form that might be mastered. At its heart, Cézanne's work is "extraordinarily attached to the firm data of vision."[16] We think of the repeated advice of Hemingway in *The Sun Also Rises* and in *Death in the Afternoon* to be unremittingly visual, to reduce suppositions to fact. One principal reason for the assertiveness of landscape in *The Sun Also Rises* may perhaps be found in art history: It "meant more than an attachment to the visible; it also meant a search for the solid form, the clear space, and the distinct outline."[17] Those things are not existentially present in Jake Barnes's life in Paris and need to be perceived for the assurance that they exist.

Hemingway understood that changing the language of prose was equivalent to Cézanne's changing the "language" (he himself called it the "text") of visualization.[18] What did either one of them want to accomplish? Here is a somewhat stressed comparison of pictorial intentions. The first passage reflects the rediscovery of "social values" by impressionist scholarship toward the end of the twentieth century. It tends to impose revisionist ideology on painting.[19] The second was published during Hemingway's lifetime, when standards emphasized form and technique:

> The Impressionists had discovered nothing less than a language more significant than matter. Each painter in his own way was transforming "content" (state, ideologies, politics, social thought) into intangibles such as light, shade, color, ambivalent forms that blurred representation. A purple tree in Van Gogh and Gauguin, forerunning Matisse and *les Fauves*, is an audacious attack upon everything the state represents. It forces a new way of visualizing, such is in itself an element of anarchy. By turning expected content into aspects of light and association, the painter has disrupted reality (one kind of language) and reconstructed it along lines ideology cannot touch (in another kind of language).[20]

> Here is a sampling of . . . depositions: Manet declared (Malraux notwithstanding) that he painted what he saw. Van Gogh's avowed aim was to be "simply honest before nature." Cézanne exclaims: "Look at that cloud! I would like to be able to paint that!" And he says: "We must give the picture of what we see, forgetting everything that has appeared in the past." Even for Matisse the problem is to maintain the intensity of the canvas whilst getting near to verisimilitude."[21]

We probably are not going to adjudicate this. I note, though, that the position of the first citation can't be verified by going through Cézanne's letters, interviews, or assessments of his own work.[22] As for Hemingway, he said much about painting but he did not say anything like that. Given the tendency of art history in Hemingway's lifetime, it makes more sense to rest on Virginia Woolf's conclusion that modernist painting is based on the perception of what is actually visualized. After considering Cézanne, Roger Fry, and the twenties, Woolf judged that the entire process of reinterpreting post-impressionism was the great intellectual event between the wars. She cites Fry on Cézanne, and it requires very little imagination to realize how close language, purpose, and idea are to Hemingway: the enemies of the new art "lack the ambition to attempt those difficult and dangerous feats by which alone they could increase their resources and exercise their powers by straining them to the utmost." That is not a political problem. Woolf writes that "seeing" dispassionately was the only possible route to modern perception.[23] As for its mode, we need to recall that definition of "highly technical operation in a trade or art."

~

Meyer Schapiro commented on a late painting of Cézanne's—one of many depicting Mont Sainte-Victoire—that it was remarkable for its "intense color" and "pure tones." The series of late landscapes on this subject are characterized by color "on a vast scale."[24] It is a statement that corresponds to the practice of Hemingway, particularly to *The Sun Also Rises.* The kinds of tones matter greatly:

> There were long brown mountains and a few pines. . . . there were white cattle grazing the forest. . . . we saw a whole new range of mountains off to the south, all brown and baked-looking and furrowed in strange shapes. . . . We came around a curve into a town, and on both sides opened out a sudden green valley. . . . Far back the fields were squares of green and brown on the hillsides. Making the horizon were the brown mountains. . . . We went through the forest and the road came out and turned along a rise of land, and out ahead of us was a rolling green plain, with dark mountains beyond it. . . . The green plain stretched off. . . . As we came to the edge of the rise we saw the red roofs and white houses of Burguete.[25]

The colors are restricted to the same palette. After Burguete, there are dark browns for mountains, gray for rocks, a darker set of tones for trees, a scattering of white and red for houses—and what Hemingway describes as patches of "very green" grass between spaced trees (117). These colors are simple, but they are far more than representational.

John Rewald noted of the famed *Chateau Noir* once owned by Picasso that a bloc of yellow stands out "from a maze of green."[26] He writes of *Sous-bois provençal* that a "light green field" constitutes the foreground—and that there are almost no pictorial elements, so that "the painting is carried solely by its color." Rewald cites Theodore Reiff's observation that green is one of the four colors that dominate Cézanne's last works. The *Route tournante en sous-bois* depicts a forest whose "ocher" path winds through a forest with blue tree trunks and dense foliage whose color scheme extends from "light green to dark blue-green." In the *Route tournante* areas are "blocked in with single-tint splashes." In *Bords d'une rivière,* Rewald states, "distances are established through color modulations rather than linear devices." The view of *Chateau Noir* that used to hang in Monet's bedroom is described by Rewald in terms of "large patches" of color "densely assembled" and "interlocked." Hemingway's description of "big gray trees" and jutting "gray stone" should be viewed, literally enough, through Max Raphael's influential study of *Le Mont Sainte-Victoire vu des Lauves.* In this oil on canvas, two of the three principal colors are "ocher, and green." The painting attempts to capture the diffusion of light through color gradations ("brighter and darker greens") that are broken by verticals and horizontals positioned on their surface. (Hemingway will use the word "brown" where art history refers to ocher; Raphael does not use the word "gray" but refers to the constant interpenetrative pattern of "dark" outlined forms).[27] Cèzanne stated that his work was a matter of "tones" and "colors," not of representational form. The critics of his work note that there are particular combinations of brown and green containing flashes of red, yellow, blue, violet, broken by verticals and horizontals of black, dark blue, and gray. Both Hemingway and Cézanne depended on color as the primary variable in their landscapes. The dominant pictorial colors—"pale greens, earth colours"—seem to have been translated from one medium to the other.[28]

Beyond similarities, it remains to be asked what color contributes to structure and to idea. Rewald states of another version of *Le Mont Sainte-Victoire vu des Lauves* that "multicolored patches gain cohesion as one steps away from their entanglement and becomes aware of directions and receding planes that convey an impression of vast spaces."[29] Herbert Read states of *Le jardin des Lauves* that "the adjustment of one area of colour to its neighboring areas of colour" becomes a way of "reconciling multiplicity with an overall unity." We may be looking at "an apparent breaking up of the flat surface of a colour area into a mosaic of separate colour-facets," but we are seeing these things "completely integrated into the picture as a whole." They become "the units that together constitute the unity."[30]

At this point, we need to be aware that the discussion of color and unity of subject can lead us—quickly—to discussion of another kind. Art criticism treats the concept of unity first in terms of technique, then in terms of meaning. Metaphysics come in by the side door. For example, in one of the great critiques on the subject of color, Meyer Schapiro first identifies Cézanne's "maximal forces of color and shape" and then describes their connection to design and meaning. Cézanne's object was, he argues, to locate once more in painting the "noble harmony" that he saw and deeply admired in Poussin: "not the method of seventeenth-century composition, but its completeness and order attracted Cézanne; in his own words, he wished to re-do Poussin from nature, that is, to find the forms of the painting in the landscape before him and to render the whole in a more natural coloring based on direct perception of tones and light." The operative ideas are those of "harmony" and "order"—Schapiro calls one Cézanne work "an ordered whole," and he means that in a philosophical and possibly even a religious sense.[31] That is not unusual even in modernist art history. There is a good summation on this point in Pavel Machotka's study of landscape. He argues that Cézanne had the usual inescapable issues of working out through his art the problems of his emotional development. He wanted to express "love, passion, jealousy, retribution, and death." The discipline of landscape allowed these feelings to find an appropriate form:

> If we assume that the contact of painted forms stands for the contact of physical ones, then the act of painting—a landscape above all—carries the promise of an ideal expression of the satisfactions from closer human relations, and also the risk of failing. However imprecisely one must formulate the connection, it seems to be there. Perhaps it could be put yet differently. Any painter who attends to formal relations creates an integrated world within his frame; the satisfaction from making the integrations "work" is deep. Surely the world one creates in this way is a symbol, even proof, of the wish for integration—that is, the wish for an inner world in which conflicts are resolved in a workable manner. That must also describe Cézanne's progression.[32]

In short, "formal relations" inexorably lead to other kinds of relations.

~

The exhibition Cézanne in Provence at the National Gallery (2006) has revived old ideas. We are accustomed to seeing his work in terms of radical innovations of form; now, at his centenary, criticism has returned to the language of art used by Cézanne and his friends. Letters, conversations, and interviews provide strong evidence that the late landscapes refer themselves to historical and even religious ideas. Cézanne's phrase the "harmony parallel to nature" may mean that he sees the terrain of Aix, especially as depicted in *La Montagne Sainte-Victoire,* allegorically. This particular landscape signifies the growth of France based upon the civilizing influence of Rome, and consequently of Catholicism. His landscape shows what he insisted was "harmony" because it is infused with history and, most important of all, with mystical feelings for Provence that he often asserted. In other words, his paintings are intended to show more than the terrain of France at the turn of century. The area around Aix was a sacred place, and the name of his mountain is *Victory.* So, one great fact of his work is that "the same subject seen from a different angle offers subjects for study of the most powerful interest." But a second is that the subject has enough allusive depth to withstand recurrence. Cézanne was, of course, deeply conscious that his landscape had been treated by other artists with "awe and devotion" for centuries. As Hemingway noted and Lillian Ross did not in their interview, there was a continuity of landscape styles and meanings. And, as he wrote in *The Sun Also Rises,* the immersion in landscape is more than a vacation for Jake Barnes. Especially, in a landscape impacted by religious imagery, containing—as landscape necessarily does—the elements of the Creation.[33]

A good deal remains to be said of this. First, however, we do need to think about the tactics of construction. Where do we locate the structures and concepts of harmony, integration, and order? "The foreground," Schapiro writes of *L'Estaque, Melting Snow* is "the observer's space" and, as in Hemingway, that is where the issue is adjudicated.[34] The natural mosaic of the Irati River in *The Sun Also Rises* is described by Jake, witnessed by Bill, recalled by an Englishman named Harris. All suggest the achievement of some kind of inclusive natural order. We go from foreground to a place "way off" where the landscape ends:

> It was a beech wood and the trees were very old. Their roots bulked above the ground and the branches were twisted. We walked on the road between the thick trunks of the old beeches and the sunlight came through the leaves in light patches on the grass. The trees were big, and the foliage was thick but it was not gloomy. There was no undergrowth, only the smooth grass, very green and fresh, and the big gray trees well spaced as though it were a park. "This is country," Bill said.
>
> The road went up a hill and we got into thick woods, and the road

> kept on climbing. Sometimes it dipped down but rose again steeply. All the time we heard the cattle in the woods. Finally, the road came out on the top of the hills. We were on the top of the height of land that was the highest part of the range of wooded hills we had seen from Burguete. There were wild strawberries growing on the sunny side of the ridge in a little clearing in the trees.
>
> Ahead the road came out of the forest and went along the shoulder of the ridge of hills. The hills ahead were not wooded, and there were great fields of yellow gorse. Way off we saw the steep bluffs, dark with trees and jutting with gray stone, that marked the course of the Irati River. (117)

Hemingway's motifs of distant hills and winding roads are recognizable within Cézanne's late landscapes.[35] There are other and equally important motifs—we recall him saying in the Ross interview that "this is what we try to do" with "the woods, and the rocks."[36] All of these are, characteristically, in the episode of the Irati, and need to be made into what Schapiro called "an ordered whole." But order is more complex than it looks. The trees in Cézanne are forms: "each line, each stroke, is coordinated with all other colored marks, both angled patches and angled lines, and the whole is developed as a single, continuing rhythm and comprehensive harmony . . . [and may well belong] to the painting rather than the landscape."[37]

There are extrapolated meanings of "harmony." When Bill Gorton says that "this is country" we are convinced that Jake's description has revealed "an ordered whole": and also that Bill's response is the only possible one. Yet, Bill may himself see the landscape differently. That is more than likely—there is no reason for his perceptions to be identical to Jake's. But Bill reacts to the landscape as Jake has described it to the reader. He *verifies* the description that Hemingway has put in Jake's mouth—although it is not photographically accurate but a translation of postimpressionism. It might be said that Bill testifies to the realism of postimpressionism. And also to the depth of feeling in allusion.

There are "woods" in Jake's description that are visualized, but not in terms used before the redefinition of color and form. Kenneth Clark says of Cézanne's landscapes that they can register even "trees in the wind" even though "there is no attempt to delineate a leaf." In spite of that, "these trees are remarkably true to nature."[38] Hemingway's trees, woods, and rocks are visually inexact—while also being visually familiar. They are frequently described: the bus going to Burguete passes through "a forest of cork oaks, and the sun came through the trees in patches." Then, there are "wooded" mountains and "the white of the road showed through the trunks of a double line of trees that crossed the plain toward the north" (108). The passages cited above, going to the Irati, keeps on reminding us of both natural facts and painterly motifs: "toward the woods on the slope at the first hill. . . . into the woods. . . . a beech wood and the trees were very old. Their roots bulked above the ground and the branches were twisted. . . . thick trunks . . . sunlight came through the leaves in light patches. . . . the foliage was thick. . . . big gray trees. . . . into thick woods . . . the range of wooded hills. . . . a little clearing in the trees" (116–17). I have by no means cited all such references, but when Hemingway wants to describe nature he seems to do so in post-impressionist terms. The same is true, as one might expect, in both parts of "Big Two-Hearted River." "Part I" describes fern and jack pines, undulations in the landscape, a pine plain, and also "a great solid island of pines" in the middle ground. Trees are everywhere, but we sense them through vertical forms and dark colors only—which is exactly what should be expected:

> There was no underbrush in the island of pine trees. The trunks of the trees went straight up or slanted toward each other. The trunks were straight and brown without branches. The branches were high above. Some interlocked to make a solid shadow on the brown forest floor. Around the grove of trees was a bare space. It was brown and soft underfoot as Nick walked on it. This was the over-lapping of the pine needle floor, extending out beyond the width of the high branches. The trees had grown tall and the branches moved high, leaving in the sun this bare space they had once covered with shadow. Sharp at the edge of this extension of the forest floor commenced the sweet fern.[39]

The passage is mainly about light and form. It is overwhelmingly visual, intensely concerned with spatiality. We see not only Hemingway's view but also Cézanne's mosaic, his interlocking verticals, his sense of light, his single tones. In fact, what we see is "the representation of form, space and light" that came to dominate impressionism.[40]

John Rewald wrote of one of the Château Noir landscapes that it shows "all the basic elements of his motif: the slope with its boulders, the curves of the tree, the denseness of the forest, and even the spot near the top through which some light penetrated this almost mysterious scene."[41] That would seem to cover Hemingway's basic elements as well. F. Novotny also emphasizes the silence ("breathless quiet") of the late landscapes, and describes the "notable density" of "the forest scenes." How do "the woods, and the rocks" relate to each other? They seem to go together in an alternation of forms, predominant among them "thick foliage" with "cross-directional accents of tree trunks and branches." They are perceived without having been composed—and they do not need composition, which is after the fact. In the late landscapes we expect to find natural detail—but "the overall rendering is summary." That is to say, things are apprehended by their mass and color. Individual trunks and branches "as well as the shapes of rocks" provide the basic vocabulary.[42] The late watercolor landscapes, according to Geneviève Monnier, refuse to "outline the contours" of objects. There are "no definite boundaries" in tree branches or leaves. The only thing that matters is light "animating the . . . surface" of trees and rocks.[43] I think that Monnier's insight should be applied to Hemingway's scenes.

What are those scenes in *both* cases? The object is to isolate and show the workings of light on natural surfaces. Rocks edge through and solidify and separate aspects of both worlds; trees exist as "woods" and also solitary trunks with branches—really verticals and horizontals throughout color zones. They show the play of form on rough curved surfaces. There are very few colors, with green and brown dominant. By far the greatest attention is paid to natural formations—although there may be buildings, cattle, or people, these play a subservient role to fields, hills, and forests. In Hemingway, landscape is big, panoramic. It is rarely tied to property but goes from one horizon to another. Roads curve endlessly through Hemingway's landscapes, exactly as in Cézanne's. That is because one is expected to traverse the area from foreground to background, and to invest it in time. Finally, as when Bill Gorton tells us what we have seen in *The Sun Also Rises,* we are intended to realize that landscape contains certain kinds of meanings, beginning with those of form and perspective. The terms imply more than simply graphic or technical meanings. At least in landscape, the problems of perceiving existence have been solved. Although some points in the landscape remain unreachable, the scene has been stabilized. We can see already that we have gone beyond the description of terrain: even beyond its appreciation as a natural phenomenon.

It is necessary in the case of Hemingway to think about the tension between what can and cannot be resolved. And to think about the correspondence of literary and painterly forms. E. H. Gombrich's "Visual Metaphors of Value in Art," published in 1954, well within Hemingway's lifetime, is based on visualization in Keats and Wordsworth. Before modern times, according to Gombrich, it was accepted that landscape reinforced feelings and insights: he reminds us that "the major key lends itself to the musician as a symbol or metaphor of gaiety . . . a stormy sky in the background of a massacre can be used as a metaphor of passionate grief." Eventually, until the advent of impressionism, both art and literature became supercharged with the desire to "paint the affects."[44] It was no wonder, then, that "lines, colours, and patterns" displaced heavily freighted symbolism. Modernism avoids emotional excess, even emotional expression: Bill Gorton's laconic admiration of the Irati valley is matched by Frederick Henry's response to the "fine country" of the Swiss mountains.[45] In short, Hemingway got rid of what Gombrich calls "illustration, representation, imitation, sentiment, contrivance."[46] But, Gombrich remarks, it is harder than it seems to abandon the idea of "value," if only because lines, colors, and patterns are themselves continually reinterpreted. *They* become new patterns of the good, noble, and beautiful. As I've noted, the history of Cézanne criticism invests just as much moral sensibility in his technique as was conferred earlier to the stupendously pedagogic works of the Academy. Gombrich points out that we cannot escape values in art. Even modernist art critics find voluminous reasons for praising nature in postimpressionism. So, it is no good at all ducking the issue—portraying landscape in painting means conveying feelings about harmony and order, while the interpretation of a particular canvas speaks to the experiencing of a particular moment in life. Even the most forward-looking of Cézanne's critics, Fry and Woolf among them, find sensibility—more than that, the entire issue of moral being—in the geometry of motifs. That is why landscape in Hemingway speaks to his readers. And also to his protagonists—although, as with Frederic Henry and the Abruzzi and Jake Barnes at Roncesvalles, they cannot listen.

5
Hemingway's Michigan Landscapes

Any study of Hemingway and painting ought at least to begin with representation. The Michigan Hemingway Society's Web site identifies locations in Horton Bay, Walloon Lake, Petoskey, and Harbor Springs that figure in the Nick Adams stories.[1] Routes, perspectives, even buildings associated with Hemingway are still extant, including the remains of the "Indian Camp" on Walloon Lake and the view across Lake Charlevoix from the Dilworth Resort at Horton Bay. A tourist Web site for Seney, Michigan, reminds us that the East Branch of the Fox River, happily much closer to downtown, is the actual site of "Big Two-Hearted River."[2] The town fathers have it right: Hemingway rearranged the landscape of this story.[3] It's been said that he enriched its geography.[4] There are reasons for that, principal among them that he understood the difference between location and landscape. The following is from an April 1919 letter inviting his friend James Gamble to visit his own part of the world: "This is a priceless place, Jim. Horton's Bay on Pine Lake about twelve miles from Charlevoix, about three hundred miles north of here. It is great northern air. Absolutely the best trout fishing in the country. No exaggeration. Fine country. Good color, good northern atmosphere. Absolute freedom, no summer resort stuff, and lots of paintable stuff. And if you want to do portraits. You shall do them. . . . It is beautiful country."[5] We don't expect Hemingway to be an art expert in 1919; and there is nothing to suggest that he is thinking beyond the conventions of realism. He has picked up information about the importance of northern light. The passage is intellectually open, resting on interpretation. But Hemingway is already aware that certain things may not be worth recording, while others demand emphasis.

Sheridan Baker concludes that Hemingway reported "fact with journalistic accuracy" while simultaneously "insisting that it is all fiction." However, Hemingway's 1924 letter to Gertrude Stein says of "Big Two-Hearted

River," "I made it all up."[6] The problem is not his indifference to fact. Landscape painting and writing are forms of translation. Michael Reynolds has written that "Indian Camp" is both more and less than an accurate rendition of place in time. It was written in Paris, influenced by Ezra Pound and Gertrude Stein, composed long after its moment, modeled on the storytelling tactics of James Joyce.[7] It was understood in the 1920s—I am thinking particularly of Edmund Wilson and John Dewey—that literature did not have to be "reportorial and transcriptive."[8] Even history can't be described in those terms, at least as seen at the mid-twentieth century by Isaiah Berlin: "a mere recital of facts is not history, not even if scientifically testable hypotheses are added to them." On the contrary, any convincing work of history concerns "our normal daily experience as human beings in relation to each other—the whole intellectual, imaginative, moral, aesthetic, religious life of men." And yet, the intuitive part of history "may not pass the scrutiny of a purely fact-establishing enquiry."[9]

Landscape is continually being reexamined, often in the terms set by Berlin's discussion of the recovery of history. Kenneth Clark's *Landscape into Art* begins by stating that the natural scene is invariably "recreated . . . in our imaginations" rather than reproduced. Painted landscape is symbolic and closely associated with our "memories and instincts." Even in modern times, the idea of landscape has moved away from that of "imitation."[10] These theories have been followed up; Simon Schama's *Landscape and Memory* explores the ways by which landscape becomes symbolic. He begins by reminding us that documentary photography is no guarantee of objectivity: there is the example of Ansel Adams who defined his view of Yosemite as "a religious idea" and stated that he meant through his work to "inquire of my own soul just what the primeval scene really signifies." Over the years, certain scenes and subjects have become imbued with values. In Renaissance painting, pastoral scenes became "a moral corrective to the ills of court and city." Herbs and flowers rebuked materialism and often had "Christian associations."[11] Even modern scenic representations are memories transformed by ideas.

Schama's three essentials of landscape are "Wood," "Water," and "Rock." He begins with forests because of the space they occupy in literature and myth; and he assigns to them the adversarial role they have fulfilled since romanticism. We know that forests have always been the scene for meditations on freedom—that is one of the great themes of Shakespeare's Arcadian comedy. Schama adds that forest is more authentic than city. It is associated with the unconscious—those "things that are buried but will not stay interred" in the mind. It is also understood to be more lasting than city, or the idea of culture itself. Forest composition is generally dynamic, showing both "growth and decomposition."[12] It is a visible source of evidence for the stages by which life passes into death, and for the return of life as well. One of the reasons why "Big Two-Hearted River" is emotionally affective is its regeneration of both man and scene. *Landscape and Memory* focuses not only on a subject but a scene whose importance was acknowledged by Hemingway, the forest of Fontainebleau. We recall that Hemingway referred to Cézanne's version of this scene, using the words "woods" and "rocks" as metaphors for writing.[13]

Schama concludes that "Wood" or forest is a painterly subject reminding us that the past is real, at least as real as our own abstracted lives. It criticizes civilization in a way that moral doctrines might find it difficult to match, placing issues within a symbolic narrative. The argument resurfaces in Thomas Strychacz's contribution to *The Cambridge Companion to Ernest Hemingway.* The story "The Doctor and the Doctor's Wife" describes a dispute about stolen logs between a white and an Indian. It seems personal, but evidently "the real point" about the logs is that "they symbolize a centuries-old expropriation of Indian land." The scene, in fact, needs to be read as a hostile view of Manifest Destiny in the nineteenth century.[14] That seems exaggerated.

The second elemental component, "Water," according to Schama, is subsumed under the opposition of "Nile" and "Jordan." Nile connotes "the whole source and faculty of creative moisture."[15] The fertile river implies not only abundance but the resonance of heaven and earth. "Fluvial myth" promises that gods and men are in concert, and that natural patterns will recur.[16] Jordan makes no such promise. Its image fills those landscapes in which things are ended or transformed. One might think of it as the flooded Mississippi in Mark Twain—or as the cold, transforming waters of the Tagliamento in *A Farewell to Arms.*

Landscape involves choice. Hemingway's 1919 letter to his friend Jim Gamble specifies water but leaves out a lot that isn't "paintable stuff." Choice has consistently been a problem for American landscape artists. It may have metaphysical implications: "the Hudson Valley painters had to navigate carefully between the savagery of 'wild' scenery and the mechanical clutter of the industrial river."[17] Thomas Cole's 1836 *Essay on American Scenery* stated that while the Hudson Valley had "*natural*" advantages, not much had been done by the hand of man. The landscape had to avoid certain facts: there was simply no point in revealing what American commerce had inflicted on nature. On the other hand, Schama points out, Cole's *View from Mount Holyoke, Northampton, Massachusetts, after a Thunderstorm (The Oxbow)* shows how "a cultivated state of grace" might succeed "trackless wilderness."[18] Towns and farms become images of (opulent) pastoral innocence. We learn that "American artists became ingenious at finding ways to make the industry and enterprise an undisturbing presence in the American arcadia. George Inness managed to aestheticize the Lackawanna railroad so that it drove cheerfully at middle distance, through the verdant hills and dales, a far cry from the ominous oncoming machine on Turner's bridge. And when Sanford Gifford painted Hook Mountain on the Tappan Zee stretch of the Hudson, he took good care to choose a point of view on the west bank that would look directly south, thus concealing the clutter of sheds, brick warehouses, and jetties that stuck out from the port of Nyack into the river."[19]

The last category, "Rock," means more than the term suggests. It includes mountains and, eventually, earth itself. We already know a good deal about the mystical component of this category. In the seventeenth century there was a body of theology devoted to the inutile ranges of European mountains, which were icons of the fall of man. The romantics saw things differently, devoting a substantial amount of poetry to the sublimity of mountains. Great peaks became signs of the opposition of Nature and Culture. We can't dismiss this kind of reading—since the pioneering work of Carlos Baker, Hemingway critics have known that Kilimanjaro and the Pyrenees connote more than terrain. But "Rock" is also an element of form. It is one of the great constituents of Cézanne's landscape and it makes up a number of his titles, for example, *Rocks at Bibémus, Rocks at l'Estaque, Rocks at Fontainebleau,* and *Rocks Near the Grottoes above the Chateau Noir.* To this we add dozens of sketches of the same subjects and the entire Montagne Sainte-Victoire sequence. When we ask with Ansel Adams what landscape "signifies," we move from one kind of terrain to another. In art history, John Rewald has pointed out that "the forms of the rocks" in Cézanne "are sometimes difficult to 'read.'" The illogical masses of rocks that constitute so many of his canvases are intended to be mysteries, interruptions to the mind's regularity. They testify to the break between man and nature. They often suggest not only intelligible form but inaccessibility. The largest of Cézanne's conceptions of this element, the Montagne Sainte-Victoire sequence, served the same purpose as those distant mountains so often described by Hemingway. As Rewald points out, such subjects are obsessively important to the mind, reappearing constantly as motifs.[20]

~

Two years after the Lillian Ross interview with Hemingway at the Metropolitan Museum, Meyer Schapiro stated that the ideas behind modern painting were also those of science and philosophy—and could be seen "dominating literature too." He thought that Americans were unusually hospitable to modernist landscape. That was because our own landscape painters were heavily influenced by impressionism, especially by its "light" and "atmosphere." They led their audience to "the art of a Cézanne, a Bonnard, a Vlaminck, a Marquet." And they were known, as in the case of Ryder, to be masters of the physical and emotional effects of "large mysterious patterns of light and dark." Hemingway's own depictions allude often to the problems created by modernist landscape. Such paintings often have a "mysterious" atmosphere and indefinite or "shapeless" form.[21] They will depart from the values as well as the techniques of realism.

From "Up in Michigan" to "The Light of the World," the northern Michigan stories cover more than a decade. The first of these stories names its characters, then depicts a landscape in perspective: "Hortons Bay, the town, was only five houses on the main road between Boyne City and Charlevoix. There was the general store and post office with a high false front and maybe a wagon hitched out in front, Smith's house, Stroud's house, Dillworth's house, Horton's house and Van Hoosen's house. The houses were in a big grove of elm trees and the road was very sandy. There was farming country and timber each way up the road. Up the road a ways was the Methodist church and down the road the other direction was the township school. The blacksmith shop was painted red and faced the school."[22] This is the narrator's landscape. It lets us know that there is, so to speak, a "here" and a "there" in the depiction. Five houses between two towns—this place really is a speck on the map. Yet, everything in it is known and has a relationship in time as well as place to every other thing. The roads, which figure so often and so powerfully as motifs in Hemingway, depart quickly from our visual certainties. The elements are earth and wood. Color is sparse and conceptual. The blacksmith shop is painted red—has Hemingway been reading *Tess of the d'Urbervilles?* The shop should be easily visible from the school. The next part of the narration is a different landscape seen by Liz: "A steep sandy road ran down the hill to the bay through the timber. From Smith's back door you could look out across the woods that ran down to the lake and across the bay. It was very beautiful in the spring and summer, the bay blue and bright and usually whitecaps on the lake out beyond the point from the breeze blowing from Charlevoix and Lake Michigan. From Smith's back door Liz could see ore barges way out in the lake moving toward Boyne City. When she looked at them they didn't seem to be moving at all but if she went in and dried some more dishes and then came out again they would be out of sight beyond the point" (82). This intentionally reminds us of a framed picture, possibly a rotogravure. It contains what Liz perceives in real time between doing dishes. It has emotional meaning—movement and colors dominate. The scene is more tactile than the preceding. Its elements are air and water. We might call what she sees a natural perspective—and in this story, as in all landscape, pictorial values imply other values. What she sees is clearly defined, neatly divided into planes. It is a logical scene with a dominant foreground: the objects she sees are referred (twice) to her viewpoint at "Smith's back door." The background—"way out"—is unthreatening: things move but stay the same. Location means permanence. In more than one sense of the term her perspective provides a form of order.

By the time of "The Light of the World," the idea of order had been foregone. In this story, Nick Adams and a friend go to a bar and then to a railroad station. They are famously adrift among white men, Indians, whores—and recent American history. Each group of characters is hostile to the others; and whatever is said in this story breeds argument. The dialogue undermines memory and motive. Critics have often assessed this story in terms of religious morality: "Hemingway surely was, among other things, deploring the betrayal of Christian love in our culture. . . . Hemingway, as his mother's son, was aware of the Christian suggestions in his title, but also as his mother's son, he very much realized that his views of life and art had moved beyond them. . . . The world Nick walks through is anything but Christian. . . . This is a place of illusion and contradiction. . . . the whole landscape suggests the underworld."[23] The critical history of this story provides too many answers for them to be able to sustain each other. The story may refer to a Holman Hunt painting titled *The Light of the World,* which is to say that it deals with outworn Victorian sentimentality. Certain passages in the New Testament may provide a silent commentary on its events. The scene may be a Dantean *Inferno* because Nick has (in a previous story) said that things have gone to hell with him. I doubt that this story represents the underworld or that it expresses disappointed unbelief—or that the Michigan stories operate in a direct sequence. We know that they depict an immoral world, but that is a premise, not a conclusion. Yet an important point has been made: the passage identifies this story as a "landscape" in which "contradiction" is a central theme.

Certain kinds of landscape reveal and even cause dissonance. Here is the opening perspective of "The End of Something":

> In the old days Hortons Bay was a lumbering town. No one who lived in it was out of sound of the big saws in the mill by the lake. Then one year there were no more logs to make lumber. The lumber schooners came into the bay and were loaded with the cut of the mill that stood stacked in the yard. All the piles of lumber were carried away. The big

> mill building had all its machinery that was removable taken out and hoisted on board one of the schooners by the men who had worked in the mill. The schooner moved out of the bay toward the open lake carrying the two great saws. . . . Its open hold covered with canvas and lashed tight, the sails of the schooner filled and it moved out into the open lake, carrying with it everything that had made the mill a mill and Hortons Bay a town. (105)

While we don't accuse Hemingway of knowing about art in 1919, by 1924 he knew a great deal. I don't mean his talks with Gertrude Stein in Paris or even the knowledge he gained of the postimpressionists at the Luxembourg. In the interview with Ross, he stated that "the early painters" mattered greatly to him.[24] A. E. Hotchner wrote that "the Prado contained the paintings which Ernest admired beyond all others." Some paintings he knew from his "prodigious reading," others from repeated viewing of "particular canvases." At the Prado, he discussed with Hotchner ideas and techniques of Titian, Veronese, Bosch, Botticelli, Andrea del Sarto, and Velázquez.[25] Emily Watts makes some identifications: "those painters whom Hemingway most liked" included Goya (*The Third of May*), El Greco (*Toledo*), Bosch (*Garden of Earthly Delights*), and Brueghel (*The Harvesters*).[26]

"The End of Something" is certainly based on early painterly themes because its title tells us so. I have in mind the motif of "endings" common in landscape from Poussin to Cézanne. In the opening perspective we get the sense of more than one ending. Logging is over as an industry and Hortons Bay is no longer a town. The sailing away of the ships is itself a death motif—we see them silently heading west into the open lake.[27] The land left behind is now in ruins, swampy and "deserted."

That combination of wild nature and civilized ruins is the conventional subject of elegiac landscape. The characters within the frame are young men and women—they used to be nymphs and shepherds—in love.[28] It is not a jarring allusion when we think of their modern incarnation in "The Waste Land" two years before the publication of "The End of Something." Eliot wrote that the nymphs are departed from the waters, and their lovers as well. With them, Hugh Kenner adds, is the "gone harmonious order" of the past.[29]

Love in the landscape of Eliot, Hemingway, and also Cézanne occurs within the natural cycle. That is no different from elegy. Human chronology emphasizes the temporary; natural chronology enfolds that. But the two forms of time diverge:

> "There's our old ruin, Nick," Marjorie said.
> Nick, rowing, looked at the white stone in the green trees.
> "There it is," he said.
> "Can you remember when it was a mill?" Marjorie asked.
> "I can just remember." Nick said. (108)

We have seen the situation before. Erwin Panofsky's famous essay on landscape, "'*Et in Arcadia Ego,*'" establishes the immense age of elegiac landscape, tracing it from its early sources in Virgilian poetry to the canvases of the late Renaissance. Nature is the scene of time's passing, and, necessarily, of "human suffering." Elegiac landscape likens the passing of love to the approach of death. It implies emotional and also moral "dissonance."[30] As I've noted, the title of Hemingway's short story refers to the motif of "endings." In fact, a reasonably literal title for the entire genre of elegy has already been provided by the Shakespearean phrase "remember mine end."[31] But the point is considerably larger than this tangency implies. The late landscapes of Cézanne recently exhibited at the National Gallery have been classified under the title used by Panofsky: "*Et in Arcadia Ego.*" We know how powerfully those particular landscapes affected Hemingway. I will defer discussion briefly, noting here only that the "ominously deep" colors of paintings admired by Hemingway were associated by Cézanne with new ways of looking at life and death.[32]

In Hemingway's story, as in the landscape of ruins, nature lasts longer than love—and love, with its involuntary ending, is a reminder of death. Given Hemingway's family background, it is understandable that critics have turned to the religious life of Oak Park, Illinois, and its congregational sermons, publications, and exhortations based on the New Testament for insights into morality. But there is a direct source for Hemingway's *artistic* and *philosophical* ideas in the Old Testament. Before they became elements of landscape, the elements of the Creation were dry land and water, darkness and light. There was an essential logic in their relationship—opposites are in Genesis separate or "divided" from each other. Enclosure is one of our first metaphors, while confusion is associated with chaos. The word "good" in Hemingway signifies that things are appropriate or within the limits of their natural character. In Genesis, the word "good" is applied to the disposition of things. If we were to draw a landscape of the Creation—and how often has that been done in the history of art?—we would see earth not barren but productive, waters not flooding but "gathered together unto one place"; and "lights in the firmament of the heaven to divide the day from the night."[33]

Kenneth Clark states that "Ideal Landscape" has in the past suggested the imaginative qualities of classicism. It has often depicted "harmony between man and Nature." It even suggested (and here we think of the way that landscape is perceived at the beginning of "Up in Michigan") a version of primitive innocence. The problem, according to Clark, is that our own worldview needs a new sense of landscape. Such a view necessarily shows uncertainty and instability. It states that Nature is by no means understood—and may even be beyond the power of truthful description. So we expect modern versions of nature to be fluid rather than static: and elements of our imagination, like elements of landscape, to have become distorted. "We have even lost faith," Clark wrote, "in the stability of what we used hopefully to call 'the natural order.' "[34] The last phrase has great resonance. In "A Clean, Well-Lighted Place," the older waiter knows that "nada," or "nothing"—we know it originally as chaos, a void without form—must be offset by the design of "order" (383).

How do we interpret scene and subject? The Michigan Hemingway Society and tourist Web sites refer to houses, churches, bridges, stores, and resorts as if these locations were permanent. But only at the beginning of the Nick Adams stories, in the panoramic view of "Up in Michigan," do we have that confident view of landscape. After that, these subjects recede. Mark Twain provided a number of examples of the landscape of "civilized" terrain. For instance, in *Puddn'head Wilson* the town of Dawson's Landing is described in terms of gardens, buildings, and property lines along the great river. There is a replicated geometry of flowerbeds and fence palings within the larger design; everywhere are borders, fringes, and ledges. Inevitably, "margin, perimeter, and facade" take on psychological meaning. Intuitively, we guess that "Twain's hamlet itself is entirely on an edge. For all its willed coziness, Dawson's Landing is altogether a *shore* thing."[35] That is to say, terrain implies consciousness. The town is a matter of limits, quickly reached, and also of barriers to action and thought. To pass through the river is to understand the disquietudes that are masked by civilization.

In Hemingway, earth and water are mixed in the form of marsh and swamp; air and water combine to take the form of mist. "Darkness," a word he uses with great frequency, dominates the perimeter of light. Hemingway's boundaries do not separate with biblical clarity. Edges, riverbanks, and marshlands appear with more than geographical probability. It has been pointed out that they have a "dominant meaning" of sexual awakening, often of transgression.[36] In "Up in Michigan," Liz is seduced, then walks "over to the edge of the dock" to look down at the water. There is nothing to see because "there was a mist coming up from the bay . . . and a cold mist was coming up through the woods from the bay" (85–86). In "The End of Something," events take place in "the swampy second growth" (107) when "it was not quite dark" (109). "Indian Camp" begins at twilight "in the mist." Crossing the lake, Nick is "in the mist all the time" (89).

Mist hides colors in Hemingway's landscapes. The effect is not idiosyncratic—the tendency to diffuse light and suppress color had been the subject of critical debate since the advent of impressionism. We know that Cézanne used bright colors for some overpowering paintings, but in others they appear among masses of brown and green.[37] The Barbizon school—known for depictions of the forest of Fontainebleau—used "low-keyed colors" that defied general ideas about the picturesque. Corot especially was known for the use of "misty light" at dawn and dusk.[38] Monet and others had become known for causing "diffuse effects of light" in landscape. They depicted shade and the effects of light on "absorbent surfaces." They practiced and were often accused of producing "blurred effects" that seemed "unnatural and disconcerting."[39] That is a much larger issue than may first appear. Monet famously said that he had the choice of seeing things as others did or perceiving "the exact colour and shape, until it gives your own naive impression of the scene before you."[40] The heart of the matter is that technique in landscape is closely connected to the idea of meaning in nature. The impressionists themselves were not often so boldly declarative, but their critics certainly were. And Hemingway came to the study of painting in the backwash of the conflict.

Cézanne's Fontainebleau, according to Schapiro, depicts nature in a state of "confusion," "ruins," and "chaos"—terms all taken from Flaubert's own description of the forest.[41] Critics who preferred concepts of harmony and clarity deplored the failure "to reproduce the appearance of a scene."[42] They noted the "lack of design in the landscapes of the Barbizon painters" as well as in the work of Cézanne.[43] But, as Proust wrote, painters "can alter the appearance of the visible world," while novelistic style is "the transformation that the writer's mind imposes on reality."[44] At first, in the letter of 1919, Hemingway describes northern Michigan as "fine country" and "beautiful country." In detail, "it is the most comfortable kind of fishing I have ever found. When we feel like doing trout fishing, we can fish any one of the half hundred good streams. . . . it's a great life up there just lazing around the old point and always have a line out or so for rainbow. There are trips . . . to the old Indian missions and some beautiful trips."[45] Kenneth Clark calls this attitude in painting "soft primitivism." It characterizes landscape painting until the early nineteenth century, and is not only idealized but devoted to a vision of "intellectual order" generally absent from experience.[46] That is very much the view of Hemingway's nature stated by the tourist Web sites of northern

Michigan. Streams are "picturesque." As for those beautiful trips, "you can easily travel anywhere in the Upper Peninsula." Even the trout comply with the vision of order: "natural production is more than sufficient to maintain good population." All you have to do in Seney, Michigan, is get there early.[47]

Hemingway revised his ideas about art considerably in the early 1920s. He asserts the pictorial values of impressionism and its associated schools. For example, "Indian Camp" shows us light confused with darkness and earth with water; "The End of Something" begins at twilight; "The Three-Day Blow" takes place near a meadow and we can hear guns "in the swamp" (125). In "The Battler," "the smooth roadbed like a causeway went on ahead through the swamp. . . . The swamp was all the same on both sides of the track" (130). There seems to be the same relativity between reason and insanity in this story as there is between water and earth. In "Big Two-Hearted River," we can barely see "in the almost dark" and the swamp is covered by mist (216). The swamp is omnipresent in this story, both as a natural feature and as a cathexis or investment of emotional significance in the mind. In "Ten Indians," Nick walks at night through farmland by paths and over fences, then descends "through a ravine, his feet wet in the swamp mud," before a psychic return, going uphill to reality (334). As in "The Battler," straight lines are superimposed on land temporarily sustaining them.

What do we make of the details? Richard Shiff explains "the tendency of a Cézanne picture to be organized by a self-generating, self-sustaining 'motif.'" It shows something that is on the artist's mind—according to the cubist Jean Metzinger, an "expression of our sentiment." What we see in a landscape may well be geologically there—but it may also "belong to the painter," be a state of mind. Shiff points out that in Cézanne—and in the varied arts of modernism that followed him—"the 'motif' never functioned as illustration. By extending its sense of specificity, some critics even opposed the 'motif' to all *visual* models, whether picturesque views taken directly from nature or patterned after images from the history of art. The 'motif' was something distinctively other, something unique."[48]

In these "canvases" the battle between ideas is already over: impression and perception are far more important than the rendering of exact detail. Light is mixed. Boundaries are uncertain. Forms are indistinct. Light and atmosphere matter more than reproduced objects. Emotion proceeds not from the subject but from its existential treatment. The power of subjectivity is enormous. It looks as if every aspect of art that the critics of impressionism wanted to annul is not only *present* but *dominant* in Hemingway's modernist landscapes. His landscapes are as much arguments as memories.

Yet, inevitably, we want to know the truth. Can there possibly have been so many swamps around Hortons Bay? Did Hemingway write down his experiences only at twilight—and does that account for the dark coloration of his work? Such questions do encumber the mind. We might think of the depiction of Paris in *The Sun Also Rises.* Cityscape in this novel reminds us of nothing so much as the landscape of streams and fields in northern Michigan. Both are metaphorically dark, full of the strains of sexual and personal dissonance. Hemingway's depictions give tactical weight to Kenneth Clark's idea that a modern landscape needs to be unideal. The experience of Cézanne as a landscape artist was, I think, on Hemingway's mind. For example, Cézanne's landscape of Provence is not painted in terms of ideal forms. In fact, it is somewhat aesthetically disappointing. Cézanne took as his subjects trees living and dying, rocks jumbled together in great irregularities, houses and mills past any rational use. The paintings do not try for pathos, and they do not give a false sense of order. The idea of design is subordinated to the vagaries of nature and the truths of the passage of time. It was a landscape that included and even anticipated death. John Rewald wrote that many of the subjects included in these canvases—"facades withering under the persistent mistral"—are about a history already over by the late nineteenth century.[49] Even in Provence, life is not understood, and Nature seems to repel analysis.

There is a final issue, one that was highly important for Hemingway. His business was to change writing itself. We know that the subjects Cézanne painted had been done by other artists before he appropriated them. Theories of landscape had emphasized the creation of "an exactly true effect." That meant we expected to see a "scientifically exact landscape portrait." Quite literally, Cézanne brought an end to false ideas about "scientific perspective." Nor would there be any more quaintness of regionalism. He had a proprietary conception of the Aixois—in fact, as his reputation grew, he was said to have "retaught today's painters" of that place.[50] That says something of Hemingway's idea of his own function as a writer.

Notes

Introduction

1. Fitzgerald, "My Generation," in *My Lost City*, 194. See Robert Roulston, "'The Swimmers'; Strokes against the Current," in Bryer, *New Essays on F. Scott Fitzgerald's Neglected Stories*, 156–57, for "themes" and "problems" of the twenties in Fitzgerald's work.

2. See Bruccoli, *Some Sort of Epic Grandeur*, for discussion of Fitzgerald and behaviorism (237); his theory of anxiety and emotional bankruptcy (289–90); Zelda's schizophrenia (291–304); Fitzgerald's theory about the mental effects of physiology (308); the proposed psychiatric treatment for Zelda and himself as "a joint case" (342); the "neurasthenic condition" of both Scott and Zelda (345–52); the psychological history of the Sayre family (479).

3. Ibid., 365: "Fitzgerald was particularly pleased by the review [of *Tender Is the Night*] in the *Journal of Nervous and Mental Disease*, which stated that the novel was 'an achievement which no student of the psycho-biological sources of human behavior, and of its particular social correlates extant today, can afford not to read.'"

4. Fitzgerald, *The Short Stories of F. Scott Fitzgerald*, 35, 39. Future references to this volume will be cited parenthetically in my text.

5. Curnutt, "F. Scott Fitzgerald, Age Consciousness, and the Rise of American Youth Culture," 32–33.

6. Fitzgerald, *The Beautiful and Damned*. I have used the Penguin edition cited in the bibliography because its text is on the Internet. In this passage I have given the page references parenthetically in my text. I am grateful to Ruth Prigozy for pointing out the high incidence of the word "drift" in this novel.

7. See the discussion of James in Berman, *Fitzgerald, Hemingway, and the Twenties*, 12–15.

8. See Westbrook, *John Dewey and American Democracy*, 294: "Lippmann did not rely on Freudian or behaviorist conceptions of human nature but on psychological and philosophical premises similar to those of Dewey and William James."

9. Lippmann, *Drift and Mastery,* 331–33.

10. Wilson, *I Thought of Daisy,* 125.

11. Walter Lippmann, *Public Opinion* (New York: Free Press, 1997), 71–72.

12. Mencken, "The Advent of Psychoanalysis," in *H. L. Mencken's Smart Set Criticism,* 147–49.

13. Freud, "Creative Writers and Day-dreaming," in *The Freud Reader,* 440.

14. See Edmund Wilson's letter to Fitzgerald (July 31, 1922) on the fallacies of the "controversy about the Younger Generation" in his *Letters on Literature and Politics,* 88.

15. Fitzgerald, "Introduction to the Modern Library Reprint of *The Great Gatsby,*" in *F. Scott Fitzgerald on Authorship,* 140.

16. Fitzgerald, *A Life in Letters,* 130.

17. Ibid., 139.

18. Ibid., 119; 123.

19. See Santayana, *Reason in Society,* 164.

20. Lippmann, *Public Opinion,* 104.

21. Dewey, "Search for the Great Community," in *The Philosophy of John Dewey,* 642–43.

22. Westbrook, *John Dewey and American Democracy,* 336–37.

23. This letter cited by Rovit and Waldhorn in *Hemingway and Faulkner,* 39–40.

24. Nafisi, *Reading Lolita in Tehran,* 127. See Edmund Wilson's letter to Fitzgerald (April 11, 1925) in *Letters on Literature and Politics,* 121: "Your book [*The Great Gatsby*] came yesterday and I read it last night. It is undoubtedly in some ways the best thing you have done—the best planned, the best sustained, the best written. In fact, it amounts to a complete new departure in your work. The only bad feature of it is that the characters are mostly so unpleasant in themselves that the story becomes rather a bitter dose. . . . you will admit that it keeps us inside the hyena cage."

25. See Peter Reed, "Common and Uncommon Things," in Elderfield et al., *ModernStarts,* 297.

26. Ibid., 302.

27. John Elderfield, "Seasons and Moments," in Elderfield et al., *ModernStarts,* 187.

28. Dorothy Kosinski, "American Genius," in Rothschild, *Making It New,* 200.

29. Linda Patterson Miller, "Gerald Murphy in Letters, Literature, and Life," in Rothschild, *Making It New,* 158.

30. Fowlie, "On Writing Autobiography," 163–70.

31. Fussell, "Literary Biography and Its Pitfalls," in *The Boy Scout Handbook,* 79–88.

32. James, "The Self," in *The Philosophy of William James,* 124–57.

33. Spacks, "Stages of Self," 55.

34. See James L. W. West III, "Polishing Up 'Pampered" and his edited text of "The Most Pampered Men in the World," *F. Scott Fitzgerald Review* 5 (2006): 3–27.

35. Fitzgerald, *A Life in Letters,* 409.

36. Edmund Wilson, *The Twenties,* ed. Leon Edel (New York: Farrar, Straus and Giroux, 1975), 60.

37. Fitzgerald, "My Lost City," in *My Lost City,* 110.

38. See the short history of impressionist criticism by House in *Impressionism,* 207–16. In addition see: Rubin, *Cézanne;* Rewald, *The Paintings of Paul Cézanne;* Thomson, *Impressionism;* Conisbee and Coutagne, *Cézanne in Provence;* Lewis, *Critical Readings in Impressionism.*

39. Richard Shiff, "Mark, Motif, Materiality: The Cézanne Effect in the Twentieth Century," in Lewis, *Critical Readings in Impressionism,* 287–88.

40. This statement by the nineteenth-century art critic Edmund About cited by John House, "Framing the Landscape," in Lewis, *Critical Readings in Impressionism,* 87.

41. Cited by John Rewald in Rubin, *Cézanne,* 404.

42. House, "Framing the Landscape," 87.

43. See Linda Nochlin, "Seurat's *Grande Jatte:* An Anti-utopian Allegory," in Lewis, *Critical Readings in Impressionism,* 253–69.

44. Hemingway, *The Sun Also Rises,* 93–108.

45. Shiff, "Mark, Motif, Materiality," 307.

46. Clark, *Landscape into Art,* 223.

47. Cited by Rewald in Rubin, *Cézanne,* 404

48. Cited by House, *Impressionism,* 150.

49. Hemingway, *The Sun Also Rises,* 117.

50. Hemingway, "Big Two-Hearted River: Part I," in *The Short Stories,* 213.

51. Hemingway, *The Sun Also Rises,* 117.

52. Cited by Rewald in Rubin, *Cézanne,* 404.

53. Schapiro, *Paul Cézanne,* 12, 16.

54. See Machotka, *Cézanne,* 9, 13.

55. Clark, *Landscape into Art,* 1.

56. Ross, "How Do You Like It Now, Gentlemen?" 36.

57. Ibid.

Chapter 1

1. Wilson, *Letters on Literature and Politics,* 212; emphasis added.

2. Freud, *The Freud Reader,* xxii–xxiii.

3. See Lippmann, "Sigmund Freud," in *Public Persons,* 48. (First published in the *New Republic* April 17, 1915). "When I compare his work with the psychology that I studied in college, or with most of the material that is used to controvert him, I cannot help feeling that for his illumination, for his steadiness, and brilliancy of mind, he may rank among the greatest who have contributed to thought. . . . there were people who welcomed Darwin, and saw how profoundly he must affect our thinking. In Freud I believe we have a man of much the same quality, for the theories that have grown from his clinic in Vienna have . . . [affected] anthropology through edu-

cation to social organization, from literary criticism to the studies of religions and philosophies."

4. See Ronald Berman, "Fitzgerald: Mapping Progress," *F. Scott Fitzgerald Review* 1 (2002): 16–29, esp. 25–28.

5. Edmund Wilson, "The Progress of Psychoanalysis," *Vanity Fair*, August 1920, 41, 86. See the extensive coverage of *The Interpretation of Dreams* and literature in Thomas, *Dreams of Authority*, 17–69.

6. See Hobson, *Mencken*, 198–99.

7. Mencken, "The Advent of Psychoanalysis," in *H. L. Mencken's Smart Set Criticism*, 148.

8. Ibid., 149.

9. Ibid., 150.

10. Mencken, "The Critical Process," in *A Mencken Chrestomathy*, 436. For Mencken's thoughts on the psychological implications of social life in America, see the sections in the book "Democracy" (154–68) and "Americans" (169–83).

11. West, *The Perfect Hour*, 96.

12. Ibid., 126.

13. Mencken observed that *Survey* magazine (June 15, 1922) advocated the substitution of diagnostic for moralistic language: "*habit-disease* for *vice*, *psycho-neurosis* for *sin*, *failure to compensate* for *disease . . . psychopathic hospital* for *insane asylum*." The definition of "criminals" was to be changed to "*psychopathic personalities*" (*The American Language*, 292–93).

14. West, *The Perfect Hour*, 125–41.

15. Ibid., 141.

16. The phrase comes from "Jacob's Ladder," in Fitzgerald, *The Short Stories*, 364.

17. Freud, "Creative Writers and Day-dreaming," in *The Freud Reader*, 440.

18. Fitzgerald, *The Beautiful and Damned*, 234.

19. West, *The Perfect Hour*, 91.

20. Freud, "Creative Writers and Day-dreaming," 439.

21. Thomas, *Dreams of Authority*, 22–23.

22. I have used the version of "Winter Dreams" originally published in *Metropolitan* magazine in December 1922. Reprinted in West, *The Perfect Hour*, 156–82. Future references to this volume will be cited parenthetically in my text.

23. Freud, "Creative Writers and Day-dreaming," 440–41.

24. Freud, "An Autobiographical Study," in *The Freud Reader*, 29.

25. Ibid., 40.

26. Fitzgerald, *The Beautiful and Damned*, 187.

27. Santayana, *Character and Opinion in the United States*, 108–9.

28. Fitzgerald, "Where the French Outclass Us," in *Conversations*, 81.

29. Sigmund Freud, "Repression," in *General Psychological Theory*, ed. Philip Rieff (New York: Collier, 1963), 115.

30. The phrase comes from "The Rich Boy," in Fitzgerald, *The Short Stories*, 336.

31. Mencken, "The Advent of Psychoanalysis," 147–49.

32. Wilson, "The Progress of Psychoanalysis," 41, 86.

33. Santayana, *Character and Opinion in the United States,* 112–13.

34. Freud, "Creative Writers and Day-dreaming," 439–40.

35. Ibid., 442.

36. Martin, "Tamed or Idealized," 159–72.

37. Freud, *Civilization and Its Discontents,* 36.

38. James Strachey, Editor's introduction to Freud, *Civilization and Its Discontents,* 6–7.

39. Peter Gay, "Sigmund Freud: A Brief Life," in Freud, *Civilization and Its Discontents,* xx.

40. Freud, *General Psychological Theory,* 16.

41. Freud, *Beyond the Pleasure Principle,* in *The Freud Reader,* 604.

42. Freud, *Civilization and Its Discontents,* 37–38.

43. Freud, *The Ego and the Id,* in *The Freud Reader,* 658.

44. Fitzgerald, "Sherwood Anderson on the Marriage Question," in *F. Scott Fitzgerald on Authorship,* 84. Originally published in the *New York Herald,* March 4, 1923.

45. Freud, *The Interpretation of Dreams,* 392, 401.

46. West, *The Perfect Hour,* 133.

Chapter 2

1. Nafisi, *Reading Lolita in Tehran,* 96–97. (The source is *Amnesty International Newsletter* 12 [July 1982].

2. Ibid., 127.

3. Fitzgerald, *The Great Gatsby,* 57.

4. For Nick's "morally ambiguous role," see C. W. E. Bigsby, "The Two Identities of F. Scott Fitzgerald," in *The American Novel in the Nineteen Twenties,* 135.

5. Nafisi, *Reading Lolita in Tehran,* 133.

6. In 1919 Mencken posed this opposition: "'Here is a novel,' says the artist. 'why didn't you write a tract?' roars the critic." "Criticism of Criticism of Criticism," in *A Second Mencken Chrestomathy,* 307. Originally published in *Prejudices: First Series* (1919).

7. See the discussion of book banning and *The Sun Also Rises* in Michael S. Reynolds, *The Sun Also Rises: A Novel of the Twenties* (Boston: Twayne, 1988), 9–11.

8. Grant Overton, "Have You Read—?" and Isabel Paterson, "Up to the Minute," in Bruccoli, *F. Scott Fitzgerald's "The Great Gatsby,"* 209–10 and 191–92. Overton concluded that Fitzgerald would be a major figure in American letters; Paterson wrote that *The Great Gatsby* ("a book of the season only") would not be read after 1925.

9. Bruccoli, *F. Scott Fitzgerald's "The Great Gatsby,"* 193, 194–96, 200–1, 197–200; 205; 208–9.

10. Wilson, *I Thought of Daisy,* 45–47.

11. See the acute discussion of this issue by Kenneth Eble, "*The Great Gatsby* and

the Great American Novel," in Bruccoli, *New Essays on "The Great Gatsby,"* 79–95. See also Wilson, *Letters on Literature and Politics 1912–1972,* 54: "Think how many remarkable American books have been published in the last year—*Main Street, The Age of Innocence, The Ordeal of Mark Twain,* and Mencken's second series of *Prejudices*—and think how they were all of them written to tell what a terrible place America is."

12. Fitzgerald, *A Life in Letters,* 105, 119, 130.

13. Ibid., 119.

14. See Bruccoli, *Some Sort of Epic Grandeur,* 3–7.

15. Brooks, *Days of the Phoenix,* 108; emphasis added.

16. Wilson, "The Delegate From Great Neck," in *The Shores of Light,* 144, 150.

17. Fitzgerald, *A Life in Letters,* 123. See F. W. Dupee, "The Americanism of Van Wyck Brooks," in Wasserstrom, *Van Wyck Brooks,* 125: "the papers he wrote for the *Freeman* in the early twenties, and in a less direct way the biographies of Mark Twain and Henry James, were an index to his opinion of the times." As for Fitzgerald's knowledge of his subject, Brooks thought all expatriates "pretty much ignored America" (124).

18. The phrase is from *The Pilgrimage of Henry James,* cited by Hoopes in *Van Wyck Brooks,* 166.

19. René Wellek, "Van Wyck Brooks and a National Literature," in Wasserstrom, *Van Wyck Brooks,* 114.

20. Mencken, "Criticism of Criticism of Criticism," 306–7.

21. Nelson, *Van Wyck Brooks,* 163.

22. Long, *The Achieving of "The Great Gatsby,"* 172.

23. Santayana, *Reason in Society,* 164; emphasis added. See also *The Sense of Beauty,* 134.

24. See Dewey, "Search for the Great Community," in *The Philosophy of John Dewey,* 642–43. See also the editorial introduction (620) on the subject of articulating democratic experience from Josiah Royce to Dewey. The process was understood at all times to go against the national grain—the issue was understood to be the insight of art against the values of ideology.

25. Wellek, "Van Wyck Brooks and a National Literature," 114.

26. Fitzgerald, "How to Waste Material: A Note on My Generation," in *My Lost City,* 79–80.

27. Cowley, *Exile's Return,* 72, 101. See especially Cowley's account of Fitzgerald and the "escape" from politics to art, 235–45.

28. Fitzgerald, "Echoes of the Jazz Age," in *My Lost City,* 130.

29. Nelson, *Van Wyck Brooks,* 169–71.

30. Douglas, *Edmund Wilson's America,* 26.

31. Wilson, *The Higher Jazz,* 50–51.

32. See Peter Reed, "Common and Uncommon Things," in Elderfield et al., *Modern Starts,* 298. See also Maria Del Carmen González, "Tables and Objects," 313–25; John Elderfield, "Objects as Subjects," 340–49.

33. Reed, "Common and Uncommon Things," 298. This citation is from the sculptor William Tucker.

34. Alfred North Whitehead, *Science and the Modern World* (New York: Macmillan, 1953), 89, 91.

35. See Mark Girouard, *The Return to Camelot: Chivalry and the English Gentleman* (New Haven: Yale University Press, 1981), 190–91.

36. John Elderfield, "Making *ModernStarts*" and Mary Chan, "The Conquest of the Air," in Elderfield et al., *ModernStarts: People, Places, Things,* 16, 256–57; Reed, "Common and Uncommon Things," 300.

37. Miller, "Gerald Murphy in Letters, Literature, and Life," 147.

38. Kenneth Wayne, "Villa America in Context," in Rothschild, *Making It New,* 194. Ezra Pound wrote to Wyndham Lewis (April 27, 1921) on connections between the arts: "I should take you, Brancusi, Picasso, and surprising as it will seem to you, Picabia, not exactly as a painter, but as a writer. He commences in *Pensées sans paroles* and lands in his last book. *J.C. Rastaquoère* and there is also more in his design stuff than comes up in reprod." *The Letters of Ezra Pound 1907–1941,* ed. D. D. Paige (New York: Harcourt, Brace, 1950), 166.

39. Vaill, *Everybody Was So Young,* 143.

40. Reed, "Common and Uncommon Things," 298.

41. See the juxtaposition of Gerald Murphy's work with Picasso, *Glass, Guitar, and Bottle,* Juan Gris, *The Syphon,* and Jean Metzinger, *The Harbor* in Deborah Rothschild, "Masters of the Art of Living," in Rothschild, *Making It New,* 32–33.

42. Daix, *Picasso,* 185.

43. Rubin, *The Paintings of Gerald Murphy,* 42.

44. Fitzgerald, *The Great Gatsby,* 107.

45. Vaill, *Everybody Was So Young,* 140.

46. Schjeldahl, "Modern Love," 75. See Rubin, *The Paintings of Gerald Murphy,* 10.

47. Rubin, *The Paintings of Gerald Murphy,* 9–10.

48. Ibid., 11: "Many of Picasso's most beautiful Neo-Classic images grew out of his sojourns at Antibes where he picnicked daily on the beach with the Murphys."

49. Ibid., 29–30.

50. Ibid., 9; emphasis added.

51. Rothschild, "Masters of the Art of Living," 59.

52. Trevor Winkfield, "The Notebook as Sketchbook," in Rothschild, *Making It New,* 138.

53. Kosinski, "American Genius," 200.

54. Rothschild, "Masters of the Art of Living," 35.

55. Schapiro, *Modern Art,* 23–24.

56. Fizgerald, *A Life in Letters,* 288.

57. John Elderfield, "Representing *People:* The Story and the Sensation," in Enderfield et al., *ModernStarts,* 44; Mary Chan and Starr Figura, "The Language of the Body," 50, in the same volume.

58. Rubin, *The Paintings of Gerald Murphy,* 11. However, note the skepticism of Richardson on this subject: *A Life of Picasso,* 222–24. See also Rothschild, "Masters of the Art of Living," 50–55.

59. Gombrich, "André Malraux and the Crisis of Expressionism," in *Meditations on a Hobby Horse,* 79.

60. Gombrich, "Art and Scholarship," in *Meditations on a Hobby Horse,* 118–19.

61. Gombrich, "The Social History of Art," in *Meditations on a Hobby Horse,* 91.

62. Trilling, "F. Scott Fitzgerald," 251–52.

63. Eble, "*The Great Gatsby* and the Great American Novel," 85.

64. Malcolm Bradbury, "Style of Life, Style of Art and the American Novelist," in *The American Novel and the Nineteen Twenties,* 33.

65. Lippmann, *Public Opinion,* 55; emphasis added.

66. Fitzgerald is cited by Rovit and Waldhorn in *Hemingway and Faulkner,* 39–40.

67. Neale Reinitz, "Edmund Wilson on the Boom Era," in Wilson, *The Higher Jazz,* xxi. Wilson, who may have had residual doubts about expressiveness, introduces a drunk at a party who explains how "the whole economic situation could be expressed in an algebraic equation" (50–51).

68. Ibid., xxvii.

Chapter 3

1. Fitzgerald, *The Great Gatsby,* 52.

2. Fitzgerald, "Myra Meets His Family," in *Before Gatsby,* 178, 183.

3. James, "The Self," in *The Philosophy of William James,* 129.

4. Horace M. Kallen, introduction to ibid., 10–11, 37–38.

5. James, "On the Notion of Reality as Changing," in *The Writings of William James,* 303; emphasis added.

6. Santayana, *Character and Opinion in the United States,* 100, 101.

7. Fitzgerald, "Head and Shoulders," in *The Short Stories,* 22. Future references to the stories will be cited parenthetically in my text.

8. Ellmann, "Literary Biography," in *Golden Codgers,* 15.

9. Spacks, "Stages of Self," 55.

10. Myers, *William James,* 363.

11. Fowlie, "On Writing Autobiography," 166.

12. Fitzgerald, "Early Success," in *F. Scott Fitzgerald on Authorship,* 160.

13. Fussell, "Literary Biography and Its Pitfalls," 79.

14. Fitzgerald, *A Life in Letters,* 369–70. The letter is dated November 11, 1938.

15. See Tomkins, "The Mind's Eye," 85.

16. Cited by Mellow in *Invented Lives,* 116.

17. Fitzgerald, "Three Cities," in *F. Scott Fitzgerald on Authorship,* 52.

18. Tocqueville, "Of Individualism in Democracies," in *Democracy in America,* 508.

19. See Mencken, *A Mencken Chrestomathy,* 180. In 1923, Fitzgerald praised Menck-

en's *The Philosophy of Friedrich Nietzsche* (1908): "10 Best Books I Have Read," in *F. Scott Fitzgerald on Authorship,* 86.

20. Fitzgerald, "The Baltimore Anti-Christ," in *F. Scott Fitzgerald on Authorship,* 45–47. Originally published in the *Bookman* 53 (March 1921), 79–81.

21. H. L. Mencken, "Politics," in Stearns, *Civilization in the United States,* 34.

22. Van Wyck Brooks, "The Literary Life," in Stearns, *Civilization in the United States,* 193.

23. Lippmann, "H. L. Mencken," in *Public Persons,* 79–80.

24. Mellow, *Invented Lives,* 121. See Fitzgerald's letter (November 17, 1920) to Rascoe in *Correspondence of F. Scott Fitzgerald,* ed. Matthew J. Bruccoli and Margaret M. Dugan (New York: Random House, 1980), 72.

25. Klein, *Rainbow's End,* 49. One of Edmund Wilson's reviews of the decade concludes that it was wrong for Americans "to reconcile themselves to a world dominated by salesmen and brokers." Among intellectuals who did so, he singles out "jazz age romantics." "Literary Consequences of the Crash," in *Edmund Wilson: Literary Essays and Reviews of the 1920s and 30s,* ed. Lewis M. Dabney (New York: Library of America, 2007), 401. Fitzgerald's protagonists are part of the economy; from Nick Carraway to Charley Wales they work in offices and sell bonds. I think that it was Fitzgerald's economic realism that made it impossible for Wilson ever to recognize him as one of the great writers of the century.

26. Spacks, "Stages of Self," 55.

27. Fitzgerald, "Pasting It Together," in *My Lost City,* 149.

28. James, "The Self," 154–56.

29. See the review of current scholarship on "performative identity" in Curnutt, *The Cambridge Introduction to F. Scott Fitzgerald,* 31–36. Curnutt states that there was in fact "a new theatricality of daily life" in the twenties, the result of constant iteration by the film industry and consumer marketing. The urgings of movie stars and ads allowed customers to think not of their real but of their "presentational" selves—the aspect of personality that they chose to display (31, 32).

30. Freud, *The Ego and the Id,* in *The Freud Reader,* 639, 643.

31. Ibid., 642–43.

32. I have used the version of "Winter Dreams" originally published in *Metropolitan* magazine, December 1922. Reprinted by West in *The Perfect Hour.* Cited passage 170.

33. See Cowley, *A Second Flowering,* 228–29.

34. See Fitzgerald, "My Lost City," 110.

35. Fitzgerald, "Early Success," 190.

36. Fitzgerald, "Winter Dreams," 168.

37. Mencken, *A Mencken Chrestomathy,* 179.

38. Fitzgerald, "Winter Dreams," 168.

39. Fitzgerald, "My Generation," 193. Both James L. West III and Matthew J. Bruccoli date this essay 1939. See Bruccoli, *Some Sort of Epic Grandeur,* 455.

40. See the discussion of Lincoln Kirstein's life by Claudia Roth Pierpont, "Prince of the City," *New Yorker*, April 16, 2007, 144.

41. Joan Acocella, "Heroes and Hero Worship," in *Twenty-eight Artists and Two Saints* (New York: Pantheon, 2007), 197. The subject of this essay and also of Pierpont (above) is Lincoln Kirstein's self-fashioning in the twenties and thirties.

42. Fitzgerald, "My Lost City," 108.

43. Cited by Mencken in *The American Language*, 602.

44. Paul Rosenfeld, "F. Scott Fitzgerald," in *The Crack-up*, ed. Edmund Wilson (New York: New Directions, 1956), 321.

45. Petry, *Fitzgerald's Craft of Short Fiction*, 156.

46. James, "The Self," 128.

47. Fitzgerald, *A Life in Letters*, 377. The letter is dated January 10, 1939.

48. Fitzgerald, "My Generation," 194.

49. John Dewey, "The Lost Individual," in Stuhr, *Classical American Philosophy*, 386–87. From *Individualism, Old and New* (1930).

50. Ruth Prigozy, "Fitzgerald's Flappers and Flapper Films of the Jazz Age," in *A Historical Guide to F. Scott Fitzgerald*, ed. Kirk Curnutt (Oxford: Oxford University Press, 2004), 156.

Chapter 4

1. Watts, *Ernest Hemingway and the Arts*, 37.

2. Carlos Baker, *Ernest Hemingway: A Life Story* (New York: Charles Scribner's Sons, 1969), 85.

3. Ibid., 132.

4. Ibid., 268.

5. Ross, "How Do You Like It Now, Gentlemen?" 36.

6. Hemingway, *A Moveable Feast*, 13. Cézanne criticism accepts reticence. Rewald could not explain *The Gardener Vallier*, an oil on canvas, and said that "where Roger Fry remained without words, this commentator must be permitted to do likewise" (Rubin, *Cézanne*, 407). Rewald refers to Virginia Woolf's account of one of Roger Fry's last lectures—when he came to a late work by Cézanne, he announced that it was "beyond any analysis of which he was capable." The audience found that adequate, even admirable, and it was for Woolf a defining moment in criticism (Woolf, *Roger Fry*, 263).

7. See Mellow, *Charmed Circle*, 62–65, 264–66.

8. Hemingway, *A Moveable Feast*, 13–16.

9. Alfred Werner, introduction to Fry, *Cézanne*, vii–viii.

10. Rewald, *Cézanne and America*, 185; 211–34.

11. Bruccoli, *The Only Thing That Counts*, 92.

12. Fry, *Cézanne*, 5–6.

13. Machotka, *Cézanne*, 10. Flaubert and Wagner may also have been subjects for illustration.

14. Rewald, *Cèzanne and America,* 99; see also 118. Zola owned Cézanne's *L'enlèvement.*

15. Clark, *Landscape into Art,* 216. The relationship with Zola was conflicted: for a brief account, see Kelder, *The Great Book of French Impressionism,* 386–87.

16. Machotka, *Cézanne,* 12.

17. Ibid., 13.

18. See Berman, "Recurrence in Hemingway and Cézanne," in *Modernity and Progress,* 67–82.

19. See the discussion of critical theories (within an important review of the history of modern impressionist criticism) by House, *Impressionism,* 212–13.

20. Karl, *Modern and Modernism,* 107.

21. Steinberg, "The Eye Is a Part of the Mind," 246.

22. See Clark, *Landscape into Art,* 219: "All art involves selection and control of natural appearances which must reflect the artist's whole temperament, and in the choice of his dominant forms Cézanne was simply expressing his own vision of nature. But in the use of these forms he was no doubt perfectly conscious of his intentions. For this strange man, whose views on life, according to M. Vollard, *were orthodox to the point of absurdity,* was, where art was concerned, a profound and original thinker" (emphasis added).

23. Woolf, *Roger Fry,* 160, 161.

24. Schapiro, *Paul Cézanne,* 124.

25. Hemingway, *The Sun Also Rises,* 93–108. Future references will be cited parenthetically in my text.

26. Cited by John Rewald in Rubin, *Cézanne,* 402. I have referred in text and notes to the titles as they are given in the sources.

27. Ibid., 399–400, 402, 403–4.

28. Clark, *Landscape into Art,* 223. Clark adds a third dominant color for late Cézanne, modulated blues.

29. Rewald, *Cézanne and America,* 405.

30. Herbert Read, *A Concise History of Modern Painting* (New York: Praeger, 1985), 18–19; cited by Rewald in *The Paintings of Paul Cézanne,* 1:544.

31. Schapiro, *Paul Cézanne,* 12, 16.

32. Machotka, *Cézanne,* 9, 13.

33. See Paul Smith, "Cézanne's Late Landscapes, or the Prospect of Death," and Philip Conisbee, "The Late Paintings of Montagne Sainte-Victoire," in Conisbee and Coutagne, *Cézanne in Provence,* 58–74 and 280–90. Cited passages 281, 283.

34. Schapiro, *Paul Cézanne,* 38.

35. Berman, "Recurrence in Hemingway and Cézanne," 74–79.

36. Ross, "How Do You Like It Now, Gentlemen?" 36.

37. Shiff, "Mark, Motif, Materiality," 290–91.

38. Clark, *Landscape into Art,* 223.

39. Hemingway, "Big Two-Hearted River: Part I," in *The Short Stories,* 212–13.

40. House, *Impressionism,* 150.

41. Rewald, *The Paintings of Paul Cézanne,* 1:520.

42. F. Novotny, "The Late Landscape Paintings," in Rubin, *Cézanne,* 110–11.

43. Geneviève Monnier, "The Late Watercolors," in Rubin, *Cézanne,* 117–18. Monnier cites the early twentieth-century art critic Emile Bernard.

44. Gombrich, "Visual Metaphors of Value in Art," in *Meditations on a Hobby Horse,* 25.

45. Hemingway, *A Farewell to Arms,* 303.

46. Gombrich, "Visual Metaphors of Value in Art," 29.

Chapter 5

1. Marek, "Hemingway-Related sites."

2. Wood, "Seney, Michigan in the Upper Peninsula."

3. Sheridan Baker, "Hemingway's Two-Hearted River," in Benson, *The Short Stories of Ernest Hemingway,* 150–59.

4. Bruccoli, *Classes on Ernest Hemingway,* 26.

5. This letter is reprinted in Griffin, *Along with Youth,* 118.

6. Baker cites the letter to Stein in "Hemingway's Two-Hearted River," 157–58.

7. Reynolds, *Hemingway,* 164–67.

8. See Berman, *Fitzgerald-Wilson-Hemingway,* 64. The phrase comes from John Dewey's "Existence, Value and Criticism."

9. Berlin, *The Sense of Reality,* 26–27.

10. Clark, *Landscape into Art,* 1, 230, 231.

11. Schama, *Landscape and Memory,* 9, 11.

12. Ibid., 56, 58.

13. See Ross, "How Do You Like It Now, Gentlemen?" 36. See Schama's brief discussion and illustrations of the Barbizon artists Theodore Rousseau (*The Forest of Fontainebleau*) and Narcise Diaz de la Peña (*The Forest of Fontainebleau*) (*Landscape and Memory,* 530, 546, 556).

14. Thomas Strychacz, "*In Our Time,* Out of Season," in Donaldson, *The Cambridge Companion to Ernest Hemingway,* 65.

15. Schama, *Landscape and Memory,* 257. The phrase is cited from Plutarch.

16. Ibid., 260.

17. Ibid., 364.

18. Ibid., 365.

19. Ibid., 367

20. John Rewald, "The Last Motifs at Aix," in Rubin, *Cézanne,* 93, 104.

21. Schapiro, "The Armory Show," in *Modern Art,* 154, 169.

22. Hemingway, "Up In Michigan," in *The Short Stories,* 81–82. Future references to the short stories will be cited parenthetically in my text.

23. Howard L. Hannum, "Nick Adams and the Search for Light," in Benson, *New Critical Approaches,* 328–29.

24. Ross, "How Do You Like It Now, Gentlemen?" 36.

25. Hotchner, *Papa Hemingway,* 186–87.

26. Watts, *Hemingway and the Arts,* 37.

27. Horton Bay is on the east side of the lake.

28. Schapiro, *Modern Art,* 7. Both "early" and much later paintings depict this kind of scene. In fact, it is important in Cézanne, whose version of *The Amorous Shepherd* brings the matter up to date. Schapiro states that *The Amorous Shepherd* is an allusion to the argument about ideal and sexual love carried on over many years by Cézanne and Zola.

29. Hugh Kenner, *The Invisible Poet: T. S. Eliot* (New York: Harcourt, Brace and World, 1959), 164–65.

30. Erwin Panofsky, "*Et in Arcadia Ego:* Poussin and the Elegaic Tradition," in *Meaning in the Visual Arts,* 300.

31. Ibid., 308–9. For application of this theme to Hemingway's Florida landscapes, see H. R. Stoneback, "'*Et in Arcadia Ego*': Deep Structure, *Paysage Moralisé,* Geomoral and Symbolic Landscape in Hemingway," *North Dakota Quarterly* (1998): 186–203.

32. See Smith, "Cézanne's Late Landscapes, or the Prospect of Death," 73.

33. Genesis 1, 9, 14.

34. Clark, *Landscape into Art,* 139, 239.

35. Doody, "Frontier and Wild Space," in *The True Story of the Novel,* 323–24.

36. Doody, "River and Pond and Reedy Marsh," in *The True Story of the Novel,* 325.

37. See House, *Impressionism,* 148–50 for discussion of the complex relationship of "colour," "tone," and "gradations."

38. Kelder, *The Great Book of Impressionism,* 33.

39. Thomson, *Impressionism,* 159, 191.

40. House, *Impressionism,* 147–48.

41. Schapiro, *Paul Cézanne,* 108.

42. "Impressionism," in Osborne, *The Oxford Companion to Art,* 564.

43. Kelder, *The Great Book of Impressionism,* 33.

44. See Conrad, *Modern Times, Modern Places,* 157. The comments on painting by Proust come from the *Recherche;* those on writing are from *Contre Sainte-Beuve.*

45. Griffin, *Along with Youth,* 119.

46. Clark, *Landscape into Art,* 109; 138–39.

47. Wood, "Seney, Michigan in the Upper Peninsula."

48. Shiff, "Mark, Motif, Materiality," 289.

49. Rewald, "The Last Motifs at Aix," 93. See Smith, "Cézanne's Late Landscapes, or the Prospect of Death," 62.

50. Benedict Leca, "Sites of Forgetting: Cézanne and the Provençal Landscape Tradition," in Conisbee and Coutagne, *Cézanne in Provence,* 52.

Selected Bibliography

The American Novel in the Nineteen Twenties. Stratford-upon-Avon Studies 13. London: Edward Arnold, 1991.

Benson, Jackson J., ed. *New Critical Approaches to the Stories of Ernest Hemingway.* Durham: Duke University Press, 1990.

———, ed. *The Short Stories of Ernest Hemingway: Critical Essays.* Durham: Duke University Press, 1975.

Berlin, Isaiah. *The Sense of Reality.* New York: Farrar, Straus and Giroux, 1996. (Originally given as a lecture at Smith College in October 1953.)

Berman, Ronald. *Fitzgerald, Hemingway, and the Twenties.* Tuscaloosa: University of Alabama Press, 2001.

———. *Fitzgerald-Wilson-Hemingway: Language and Experience.* Tuscaloosa: University of Alabama Press, 2003.

———. *Modernity and Progress: Fitzgerald, Hemingway, Orwell.* Tuscaloosa: University of Alabama Press, 2005.

Bromwich, David. "Wilson's Modernism." In *Edmund Wilson: Centennial Reflections,* edited by Lewis M. Dabney. Princeton: Princeton University Press, 1997.

Brooks, Van Wyck. *Days of the Phoenix: The Nineteen Twenties I Remember.* New York: E. P. Dutton, 1957.

Bruccoli, Matthew. *Classes on Ernest Hemingway.* Columbia: Thomas Cooper Library, University of South Carolina, 2002.

———, ed. *F. Scott Fitzgerald's "The Great Gatsby": A Documentary Volume.* Farmington Hills, MI: Gale, 2000.

———, ed. *New Essays on The Great Gatsby.* Cambridge: Cambridge University Press, 1985.

———, ed. *The Only Thing That Counts: The Ernest Hemingway-Maxwell Perkins Correspondence.* Columbia: University of South Carolina Press, 1996.

———. *Some Sort of Epic Grandeur: The Life of F. Scott Fitzgerald.* 2nd ed. Columbia: University of South Carolina Press, 2002.

Bryer, Jackson R., ed. *New Essays on F. Scott Fitzgerald's Neglected Stories.* Columbia and London: University of Missouri Press, 1996.

Clark, Kenneth. *Landscape into Art.* New York: Harper and Row, 1979. (Originally published in 1949.)

Conisbee, Philip, and Denis Coutagne, eds. *Cézanne in Provence.* Washington, DC: National Gallery of Art and Yale University Press, 2006.

Conrad, Peter. *Modern Times, Modern Places.* New York: Alfred A. Knopf, 1999.

Cowley, Malcolm. *Exile's Return: A Literary Odyssey of the 1920s.* New York: Penguin, 1979.

———. *A Second Flowering: Works and Days of the Lost Generation.* New York: Viking, 1973.

Curnutt, Kirk. *The Cambridge Introduction to F. Scott Fitzgerald.* Cambridge: Cambridge University Press, 2007.

———. "F. Scott Fitzgerald, Age Consciousness, and the Rise of American Youth Culture." In *The Cambridge Companion to F. Scott Fitzgerald,* edited by Ruth Prigozy. Cambridge: Cambridge University Press, 2002.

Daix, Pierre, *Picasso: Life and Art.* New York: Icon, 1993.

Dewey, John. *The Philosophy of John Dewey.* Edited by John J. McDermott. Chicago: University of Chicago Press, 1981.

Donaldson, Scott, ed. *The Cambridge Companion to Ernest Hemingway.* Cambridge: Cambridge University Press, 1996.

———. "Money and Marriage in Fitzgerald's Stories." In *The Short Stories of F. Scott Fitzgerald: New Approaches in Criticism,* edited by Jackson R. Bryer. Madison: University of Wisconsin Press, 1982.

Doody, Margaret Anne. *The True Story of the Novel.* New Brunswick: Rutgers University Press, 1997.

Douglas, George H. *Edmund Wilson's America.* Lexington: University Press of Kentucky, 1983.

Elderfield, John, Peter Reed, Mary Chan, and Maria Del Carmen Gonzáles, eds. *ModernStarts: People, Places, Things.* New York: Museum of Modern Art, 1999.

Ellmann, Richard. *Golden Codgers: Biographical Speculations.* New York: Oxford University Press, 1973.

Fitzgerald, F. Scott. *The Beautiful and Damned.* Edited by Kermit Vanderbilt. New York: Penguin, 1998.

———. *Before Gatsby: The First Twenty-Six Stories.* Edited by Matthew J. Bruccoli. Columbia: University of South Carolina Press, 2001.

———. *Conversations with F. Scott Fitzgerald.* Edited by Matthew J. Bruccoli and Judith S. Baughman. Jackson: University Press of Mississippi, 2004.

———. *F. Scott Fitzgerald on Authorship.* Edited by Matthew J. Bruccoli and Judith S. Baughman. Columbia: University of South Carolina Press, 1996.

———. *The Great Gatsby.* Edited by Matthew J. Bruccoli. Cambridge: Cambridge University Press, 1991.

———. *A Life in Letters.* Edited by Matthew J. Bruccoli. New York: Simon and Schuster, 1995.

———. *My Lost City: Personal Essays, 1920–1940.* Edited by James L. W. West III. Cambridge: Cambridge University Press, 2005.

———. *The Short Stories of F. Scott Fitzgerald.* Edited by Matthew J. Bruccoli. New York: Charles Scribner's Sons, 1989.

Fowlie, Wallace. "On Writing Autobiography." In *Studies in Autobiography,* edited by James Olney. New York: Oxford University Press, 1988.

Freud, Sigmund. *Civilization and Its Discontents.* Edited by James Strachey. New York: W. W. Norton, 1989.

———. *The Freud Reader.* Edited by Peter Gay. New York: W. W. Norton, 1989.

———. *The Interpretation of Dreams.* Edited by James Strachey. New York: Avon, 1965.

Fry, Roger. *Cézanne: A Study of His Development.* New York: Noonday, 1970.

Fussell, Paul. *The Boy Scout Handbook and Other Observations.* New York: Oxford University Press, 1982.

Gombrich, E. H. *Meditations on a Hobby Horse and Other Essays on the Theory of Art.* London: Phaidon, 1963.

Green, Christopher, ed. *Art Made Modern: Roger Fry's Vision of Art.* London: Merrell Holbertson and the Courtauld Institute of Art, 1999.

Griffin, Peter. *Along with Youth.* New York: Oxford University Press, 1985.

Hemingway, Ernest. *A Farewell to Arms.* New York: Charles Scribner's Sons, 1957.

———. *A Moveable Feast.* New York: Charles Scribner's Sons, 1964.

———. *The Short Stories of Ernest Hemingway.* New York: Scribner, 1995.

———. *The Sun Also Rises.* New York: Charles Scribner's Sons, 1970.

Hobson, Fred. *Mencken: A Life.* New York: Random House, 1994.

Hoopes, James. *Van Wyck Brooks.* Amherst: University of Massachusetts Press, 1977.

Hotchner, A. E. *Papa Hemingway.* New York: Random House, 1966.

House, John. *Impressionism: Paint and Politics.* New Haven: Yale University Press, 2004.

James, William. *The Philosophy of William James.* Edited by Horace M. Kallen. New York: Modern Library, 1925.

———. *The Writings of William James.* Edited by John J. McDermott. Chicago: University of Chicago Press, 1977.

Karl, Frederick R. *Modern and Modernism: The Sovereignty of the Artist, 1885–1925.* New York: Atheneum, 1988.

Kelder, Diane. *The Great Book of French Impressionism.* New York: Cross River, 1980.

Klein, Maury. *Rainbow's End: The Crash of 1929.* New York: Oxford University Press, 2001.

Kuehl, John, and Jackson R. Bryer, eds. *Dear Scott/Dear Max: The Fitzgerald-Perkins Correspondence.* New York: Charles Scribner's Sons, 1971.

Levot, André. *F. Scott Fitzgerald.* Garden City, NY: Doubleday, 1983.

Lewis, Mary Tompkins, ed. *Critical Readings in Impressionism and Post-impressionism.* Berkeley: University of California Press, 2007.

Lippmann, Walter. *Drift and Mastery: An Attempt to Diagnose the Current Unrest.* New York: Mitchell Kennerley, 1914.

———. *Public Opinion.* New York: Free Press, 1997.

———. *Public Persons.* Edited by Gilbert A. Harrison. New York: Liveright, 1976.

Long, Robert Emmet. *The Achieving of "The Great Gatsby": F. Scott Fitzgerald, 1920–1925.* Lewisburg: Bucknell University Press, 1979.

Machotka, Pavel. *Cézanne: Landscape into Art.* New Haven: Yale University Press, 1996.

Marek, Ken. "Hemingway-Related Sites in the Horton Bay/Walloon Lake/Petoskey/Harbor Springs Area." n.d. Michigan Hemingway Society. August 26, 2007. www.northquest.com/hemingway/hemsites.html.

Martin, Quentin. "Tamed or Idealized: Judy Jones's Dilemma in 'Winter Dreams.'" In *F. Scott Fitzgerald: New Perspectives,* edited by Jackson R. Bryer, Alan Margolies, and Ruth Prigozy. Athens: University of Georgia Press, 2000.

Mellow, James R. *Charmed Circle: Gertrude Stein and Company.* Boston: Houghton Mifflin, 1974.

———. *Invented Lives: Scott and Zelda Fitzgerald.* Boston: Houghton Mifflin, 1984.

Menand, Louis. *The Metaphysical Club.* New York: Farrar, Straus and Giroux, 2002.

Mencken, H. L. *The American Language.* New York: Alfred A. Knopf, 2000.

———. *H. L. Mencken's Smart Set Criticism.* Edited by William H. Nolte. Washington, DC: Gateway, 1987.

———. *A Mencken Chrestomathy.* New York: Alfred A. Knopf, 1967.

———. *A Second Mencken Chrestomathy.* Edited by Terry Teachout. New York: Alfred A. Knopf, 1995.

Myers, Gerald E. *William James: His Life and Thought.* New Haven: Yale University Press, 1986.

Nafisi, Azar. *Reading Lolita in Tehran.* New York: Random House, 2004.

Nelson, Raymond. *Van Wyck Brooks: A Writer's Life.* New York: E. P. Dutton, 1981.

Osborne, Harold, ed. *The Oxford Companion to Art.* Oxford: Oxford University Press, 1970.

Panofsky, Erwin. *Meaning in the Visual Arts.* Garden City, NY: Doubleday, 1955.

Petry, Alice Hall. *Fitzgerald's Craft of Short Fiction.* Tuscaloosa: University of Alabama Press, 1989.

Rewald, John. *Cézanne and America: Dealers, Collectors, Artists and Critics, 1891–1921.* Princeton: Princeton University Press, 1989.

———. *The Paintings of Paul Cézanne: A Catalogue Raisonné.* 2 vols. New York: Harry N. Abrams, 1996.

Reynolds, Michael. *Hemingway: The Paris Years.* Oxford: Basil Blackwell, 1990.

Richardson, John. *A Life of Picasso: The Triumphant Years, 1917–1932.* New York: Alfred A. Knopf, 2007.

Ross, Lillian. "How Do You Like It Now, Gentlemen?" In *Hemingway: A Collection of Critical Essays,* edited by Robert P. Weeks. Englewood Cliffs, NJ: Prentice-Hall, 1962. (Originally published in the *New Yorker,* May 13, 1950.)

Rothschild, Deborah, ed. *Making It New: The Art and Style of Sara and Gerald Murphy.* Berkeley: University of California Press, 2007.

Rovit, Earl, and Arthur Waldhorn. *Hemingway and Faulkner.* New York: Continuum, 2005.

Rubin, William, ed. *Cézanne: The Late Work.* New York: Museum of Modern Art, 1977.

———. *The Paintings of Gerald Murphy.* New York: Museum of Modern Art, 1974.

Santayana, George. *Character and Opinion in the United States.* Garden City, NY: Doubleday Anchor, 1956.

———. *Reason in Society.* New York: Dover, 1980. (Originally published in 1905.)

———. *The Sense of Beauty.* New York: Dover, 1955. (Originally published in 1896.)

Schama, Simon. *Landscape and Memory.* New York: Alfred A. Knopf, 1996.

Schapiro, Meyer. *Modern Art: 19th and 20th Centuries.* New York: George Braziller, 1982.

———. *Paul Cézanne.* New York: Harry N. Abrams, 1962. (Originally published in 1952.)

Schjeldahl, Peter. "Modern Love." *New Yorker,* August 6, 2007.

Spacks, Patricia Meyer. "Stages of Self: Notes on Autobiography and the Life Cycle." In *The American Autobiography,* edited by Albert E. Stone. Englewood Cliffs, NJ: Prentice-Hall, 1981.

Stearns, Harold E., ed. *Civilization in the United States.* London: Jonathan Cape, 1922.

Steinberg, Leo. "The Eye Is a Part of the Mind." In *Reflections on Art,* edited by Susanne K. Langer. New York: Oxford University Press, 1958. (Originally published in *Partisan Review* 20, no. 2 [1953], 194–212.)

Stuhr, John J., ed. *Classical American Philosophy.* New York: Oxford University Press, 1987.

Thomas, Ronald R. *Dreams of Authority: Freud and the Fictions of the Unconscious.* Ithaca: Cornell University Press, 1990.

Thomson, Belinda. *Impressionism: Origins, Practice, Reception.* London: Thames and Hudson, 2000.

Tocqueville, Alexis de. *Democracy in America.* Edited by J. P. Mayer. Garden City, NY: Anchor, 1969.

Tomkins, Calvin. "The Mind's Eye: The Merciless Originality of Jasper Johns." *New Yorker,* December 11, 2006, 76–85.

Trilling, Lionel. "F. Scott Fitzgerald." In *The Liberal Imagination.* New York: Viking, 1959.

Vaill, Amanda. *Everybody Was So Young: A Lost Generation Love Story.* Boston: Houghton Mifflin, 1998.

Wasserstrom, William, ed. *Van Wyck Brooks: The Critic and His Critics.* Port Washington, NY: Kennikat, 1979.

Watts, Emily Stipes. *Ernest Hemingway and the Arts.* Urbana: University of Illinois Press, 1971.

West, James L. III. *The Perfect Hour: The Romance of F. Scott Fitzgerald and Ginevra King.* New York: Random House, 2005.

Westbrook, Robert B. *John Dewey and American Democracy.* Ithaca: Cornell University Press, 1991.

Wilson, Edmund. *Edmund Wilson: Letters on Literature and Politics 1912–1972.* Edited by Elena Wilson. New York: Farrar, Straus and Giroux, 1977.

———. *The Higher Jazz.* Edited by Neale Reinitz. Iowa City: University Of Iowa Press, 1998.

———. *I Thought of Daisy.* Baltimore: Penguin, 1963. (Originally published in 1929.)

———. "The Progress of Psychoanalysis." *Vanity Fair,* August 1920.

———. *The Shores of Light: A Literary Chronicle of the Twenties and Thirties.* New York: Farrar, Straus and Young, 1952.

Wood, Vivian. "Seney, Michigan in the Upper Peninsula." 2000. Exploring the North: The Upper Michigan and Wisconsin Traveler. August 27, 2007. www.exploringthenorth.com/seney/index.html.

Woolf, Virginia. *Roger Fry: A Biography.* London: Hogarth, 1940.

Index